THE SUBJECTIVE SIDE
OF STRATEGY MAKING

THE SUBJECTIVE SIDE OF STRATEGY MAKING

Future Orientations and Perceptions of Executives

T. K. Das

PRAEGER

New York
Westport, Connecticut
London

Library of Congress Cataloging-in-Publication Data
Das, T. K.
  The subjective side of strategy making.
  Bibliography: p.
  Includes index.
  1. Strategic planning. I. Title.
HD30.28.D37 1986   658.4′012   86-12344
ISBN 0-275-92340-1 (alk. paper)

Library of Congress Catalog Card Number: 86-12344
ISBN: 0-275-92340-1

First published in 1986

Praeger Publishers, 521 Fifth Avenue, New York, NY 10175
A division of Greenwood Press, Inc.

Printed in the United States of America

The paper used in this book complies with the Permanent
Paper Standard issued by the National Information Standards
Organization (Z39.48-1984).

10 9 8 7 6 5 4 3 2 1

TO MY PARENTS

PREFACE

The book proposes a conception of the corporate strategy making process that recognizes the individual strategy maker as a center-stage corporate actor. This perspective is complementary to the current emphasis on the rational-analytic mode in strategy making. An individual-centered view of the strategy making process is needed to better understand the interplay between the objective factors and the subjective perceptions and values of strategy makers. It would help explain, for instance, why a top executive turnover tends to routinely result in substantive changes in corporate strategies within the same or similar economic and organizational environments.

By recognizing the centrality of the role of the individual human being (qua a corporate actor) in organizational processes, the book proposes a subjective-perceptual framework of strategy making. It is the individual who embodies the principal agency for change in organizations. "The individual," said Chester Barnard, the eminent author-executive, "is always the basic strategic factor in organization." The aggregation of individual actions determines the future course of organizational functioning. Thus it seems important to account for the cognitions and world views of the strategy makers if we are to understand the strategy making process.

An important part of the world view of strategy makers relates to the way they view the the passage of time. As strategy making is esconced along the temporal dimension, it is a significant question whether the orientation of a strategy maker toward the future has a bearing on certain aspects of the strategy making process. This is particularly relevant for strategic planning, in which individual future orientations could have a definitive role. The relevance is in terms of the eventual consensus regarding appropriate planning horizons. Another aspect is the "silent politics of time," wherein different plan implementation periods are implicitly used as negotiating currency for influencing the choice of different strategic planning objectives. The future orientation of individual strategy makers is explored in this study as an important construct in the strategy making process.

Furthermore, strategy making involves the evaluation and choice of alternative strategic actions. This selection of alternatives is dependent on the perceptions of strategy makers in regard to two basic factors. These are the planning objectives and the appropriate planning horizons for attaining those objectives. The perceptions of the strategy makers about these two factors would determine the internal planning context or milieu of the organization. This subjective appreciation of the planning milieu would impact upon the individual choices of different alternatives.

A study was carried out to examine empirically the dynamics of the two critical aspects of the role of individual strategy makers mentioned above, namely, the future orientations and the perceptions of the strategic planning milieu. The research used a large sample of executives working in two of the ten largest U.S. commercial banks, with corporate titles ranging from Executive Vice President to Assistant Vice President.

Among the significant findings of the research reported in the book are that strategy makers having a "near future" orientation tended to prefer shorter planning horizons, perceived a higher level of consensus among organizational members about planning objectives and planning horizons, and believed that relatively more "standardized" modes of decision making prevailed in the organization, when compared with the "distant future" type of strategy makers in the same organization.

The book discusses various implications of the study findings for research as well as the practice of strategy making. It demonstrates the utility of individual future orientations in understanding the role of strategy makers in "conditioning" the character of the eventual corporate strategy. In empirical terms, the study helps explain "why long-range planning is really more short-range than anyone cares to admit." The question of developing a more distant future orientation among organizational members thus becomes a salient one once we adopt a subjective view of the strategy making process. The implications are clear for the assignment of strategy makers on the basis of their capabilities for distant future thinking. For instance, an executive having a distant future orientation could be spared, by suitable placement, the gnawing dissatisfaction of having to function within the restrictive temporal ambit of short-term activities. The converse is perhaps even more damaging to an organization: by unthinkingly assigning "near future" type of strategy makers to such activities as long-range planning, all one obtains is a pedestrian, and often misleading, extrapolation of essentially near-term insights. These latter executives, it would seem, are capable of grasping only near-future phenomena.

The impetus for this book was provided by the relative neglect of the centrality of the individual in the strategy making process. Further research in the subjective tradition is obviously needed to understand the critical role of the human participant for effective strategy making. To start with, though, it is necessary to establish that a subjective approach affords fresh insights into the strategy making process. This book seeks to contribute to that crucial initial task, in conceptual as well as empirical terms.

ACKNOWLEDGMENTS

I wish to express my thanks to all the individuals who helped me in carrying out this project. I am particularly grateful to Richard Goodman and George Steiner for their encouragement and counsel. I am also thankful to Marvin Adelson, David Boje, and Oscar Grusky for their helpful suggestions.

The commercial bank executives who participated in the study have quite literally made this book possible. While I am not at liberty to reveal their identities, I do wish to record my gratitude to them. I appreciate especially the assistance of those particular executives who gave of their time and expertise to help me finalize the survey questionnaire and facilitate its service.

Finally, I am indebted to my wonderful family, whose unfailing support continues to provide me with the inspiration to reach for all that I prize.

CONTENTS

PART II: FUTURE ORIENTATIONS AND PLANNING MILIEUX

PART III: RESEARCH METHODOLOGY AND RESULTS

APPENDIXES

LIST OF TABLES

LIST OF FIGURES

LIST OF APPENDIXES

PART I
SUBJECTIVE PERCEPTIONS OF STRATEGY MAKERS

1
SUBJECTIVE DIMENSIONS OF THE STRATEGY MAKING PROCESS

THE INDIVIDUAL IN THE STRATEGY MAKING PROCESS

The traditional conception of strategy making empha-
sizes objective knowledge and rationality to the relative
neglect of the role of individual strategy makers. The subjective values and perspectives of strategy makers are
either ignored or relegated to a peripheral status. The
general assumption is that the predominantly objective content of a strategic plan would perhaps make for greater consensus among organizational members. This conventional view
holds that while executives may differ in the formulation of
specific plans, these differences are only in terms of
rational considerations regarding how best to impact upon
the objective corporate environment, and not in terms of any
inherent differences in the subjective appreciation of that
environment.

The rational-analytic or synoptic conceptions of strategy making occupy a dominant place in the literature
(Camerer, 1985; Grant and King, 1982; Greenwood and Thomas,
1981; Hax and Majluf, 1981; Radford, 1980). They are, however, not beyond question. The realities of the environment
of strategy making are not as self-evident as traditional
conceptions make them out to be (Ackoff, 1981; Morgan, 1983;
Peters, 1982;

The process of strategy making, as any other organizational process, is much dependent upon the individual cognition of the world by the organizational members (Barnard,
1938; Gardner, 1985; Simon, 1976; Weick, 1979). Strategic
decisions by individuals are the basis of change in organi-

3

zations (Child, 1972; Montanari, 1978; Weick, 1979). Organizational direction is a consequence of the aggregate of individual actions, and the cohesion of individual decisions may take place through changing coalitions or organized anarchies (Cohen, March, and Olsen, 1972; Georgiou, 1973; Leibenstein, 1979; March, 1962; Silverman, 1970). The origin, though, remains in the subjectively meaningful actions of individual organizational members (Weick, 1984). Hence, an accounting of the cognitions of the subjective environments of the organizational members is necessary for understanding the strategy making activity (Ackoff, 1981; Anderson and Paine, 1975; Davis, 1982; Goodman and Huff, 1978; Maruyama, 1982; Ronchi, 1980; Vickers, 1965). "The individual," said Barnard (1938:139), "is always the basic strategic factor in organization."

The importance of the subjective side of individual organizational members has not, however, been adequately acknowledged in the literature. There is growing evidence, though, that researchers are recognizing the role of this subjective side (Astley, 1985; Barnes, 1984; Beyer, 1981; Emshoff, Mitroff, and Kilmann, 1978; Miller, Kets de Vries, and Toulouse, 1982; Mintzberg, 1976; Sims and Gioia, 1986; Taylor, 1976; Wrapp, 1967).

Curiously, however, despite the recognition that subjective factors impinge substantively on the strategy making process, researchers have generally tended to stay with the rational-analytic conception and the traditional objective factors in their investigations. This ambivalence is evident from a perusal of the following collage of typical comments made over the last decade or so by a variety of researchers in the field:

> the action an organization takes in responding to its environment are much more likely to be consistent with top management perceptions of the environment than any "objective" indicator of environmental conditions is likely to predict. (Miles, Snow, and Pfeffer, 1974:257)

> It is difficult, if not impossible, to consider environmental effects and organization responses without considering or examining the perceptual processes of those people who are responsible for altering internal states of the firm. (Anderson and Paine, 1975:822)

"What is" is a function of both the context and
the observer. Any formulation of an "overall
design" and positive identification of its "component parts" is, therefore, relativistic with
respect to time and to the specific reflecting
minds. If one cannot operate in the world as if
there is a unique, absolute reality, then reflection and action in the real world no longer depend
on the construction of an objective theory that
describes or predicts "the truth out there." ... A
set of perceivers, each with his own image of the
world, data sources, and valuations, may hold not
only different but incompatible appreciations of
the same phenomenon, none of which can be called
the best. (Goodman and Huff, 1978:336)

Organization theorizing and research in the past
decade has, more or less by default, gradually
reduced the role of persons as significant decision makers in organizations. (Aldrich, 1979:136)

we need much more study of the managers as a variable. This person's perceptions, biases, irra-
tionalities, and style of management, to note a
few variables, have highly significant bearings on
strategic choices. A little work has been done in
this area, but we have not yet begun to appreciate
these variables in decision making let alone
understand their influence in different situations
and types of strategic decision making. (Steiner,
1979:415)

A growing body of research centres on the relationship between managerial beliefs and perceptions, and organizational survival and
performance. Although different constructs are
employed, there is some agreement that top-level
administrators derive strategies from a world view
held by a dominant coalition. These world views,
or "myths," are beliefs and postulates fashioned
into a cognitive map which to administrators is
reality. Strategic decisions are based upon this
map of reality. (Lenz, 1981:140)

beliefs are ... a powerful constraint on the
options the executives will consider and the decisions they make ... these beliefs can be so power-

> ful a constraint that top management may miss
> opportunities presented by actual or potential
> changes in the objective constraints. (Donaldson
> and Lorsch, 1983:10)

> Almost all outcomes in terms of organization
> structure and design, whether caused by the envi-
> ronment, technology, or size, depend on the inter-
> pretation of problems or opportunities by key
> decision makers. (Daft and Weick, 1984:293)

Although phrased differently, the common message is that the
perceptions and cognitions of the individual member in an
organization -- constituting what is termed here as the subjective side -- have a significant role in the organizational scheme of things (Hamel, 1980). (The organizational
members concerned with various aspects of the strategy making enterprise will sometimes be referred to as strategic
actors in this study.)

FUTURE ORIENTATIONS

An important cognitive element of the world view of all
strategic actors in an organization is the individual orientation toward the passage of time (Cottle, 1974; Fraisse,
1963). As the subject of strategy making is intrinsically
concerned with the temporal dimension (Ewing, 1972) -- especially the future time dimension --, it would seem relevant
to investigate the nature of the relationship that a strategy maker's perspective of the future could have with certain aspects of strategic planning. Specifically, it seems
a significant question as to whether this future orientation
is related in any way with the preference for particular
organizational planning horizons. The significance is in
two related areas. It is important in terms of the eventual
consensus regarding planning horizon choices. It is also
very relevant in terms of the unexplored "silent politics of
time" that pervades the negotiation of different plan implementation periods. The temporal politics is implicit in the
influencing process regarding the choice of different strategic objectives.

It is well known that individuals have an inherent orientation in regard to the passage of time (Cottle, 1976;
(Cottle and Klineberg, 1974; Fraisse, 1963; Fraser, 1981;
van Fraassen, 1978). The literature also reflects that
individuals differ in regard to whether the near or the dis-

tant future has more cognitive dominance. Goodman (1973) seems to employ a parallel notion to organizational entities, developing an organizational typology based on the two dimensions of organizational time horizon (short and long) and knowledge of the environment (meager and rich).

It therefore seems important to study the future orientations of individual executives to explore the relevance of this construct in the strategy making process.

STRATEGIC PLANNING MILIEUX

The perceptions of strategy makers regarding the nature of the environment of planning within the organization constitute another important dimension of the subjective side of strategy making. Specifically, this internal setting or context, here termed as "the planning milieu," is the matrix of the perceived degree of consensus among strategy makers concerning planning objectives and planning horizons.

The selection of specific organizational actions among alternatives is an essential element of the strategic planning process. This choice making is dictated by the perceptions of strategy makers in regard to two critical dimensions. These are (a) the organization's planning objectives and (b) the appropriate planning horizons for attaining those objectives. A strategy maker may perceive that there is complete consensus about the planning objectives among people in the organization or that there is some lack thereof. And similarly for appropriate planning horizons. Thus, dichotomizing these individual perceptions into relatively more agreement versus relatively less agreement, we have four broad types of combinations. Each of these types can be represented as a quadrant in a two-by-two matrix, with the two dimensions being the planning objectives and planning horizons expressed in terms of the relative degree of agreement perceived by individual strategy makers.

Depending, then, upon how the various combinations of planning objectives and planning horizons are perceived by the strategy makers, it is evident that the objectives-horizons matrix constituting the planning milieu within the organization will be evaluated or interpreted differently by each individual concerned. This subjective understanding of the internal organizational context or milieu of planning would impact upon the individual choices of different alternatives, including the preference for different planning horizons for strategic planning. Thus, the perception of the planning milieu would be a significant aspect to study in understanding the subjective side of strategy making.

OVERVIEW OF THE BOOK

The purpose of the study reported here is to gain some understanding of the subjective side of strategy making. This is attempted by focusing on the cognitive orientations of individual strategy makers in terms specifically of their temporal perspectives and the perceived planning milieux within an organization.

The study conceptualizes strategy making as a process in which there is a conglomeration of many strategy makers. This incidentally facilitates the examination of the impact of organizational level differences among strategy makers in the dynamics of time perspectives and perceived planning milieux.

As has been mentioned earlier, the strategic actors are considered the most significant element in the planning process. The study, in consonance with that viewpoint, examines empirically the dynamics of two critical aspects of the subjective role of the individual strategy makers, namely, the future time perspective and the perception of the planning milieu. These two aspects are considered in relation to preferences for specific planning horizons and the modes of decision making adopted in the planning process. By examining the temporal and planning milieu dimensions simultaneously, the study also seeks to explore the existence of any association between the two critical subjective aspects of strategic planning.

An important aim of the study was to investigate a "normal" population concerning strategy making, namely, top executives in the business setting of commercial banking. Also, a function which spans a major part of a corporation (here, electronic banking) was selected so that a wide range of executives was routinely involved. This served to retain for the study a certain degree of credibility that is sadly absent in many research endeavors which deal with respondent populations only remotely related, if that, to strategy making in business.

The study would be of timely interest in view of the fact that strategic planning in the fast-changing electronic banking technology is a critical activity in the banking industry today. Commercial banks in this country, perhaps more than any other type of business today, are required to contend with the tremendous advances being made in computer and telecommunications technology. In order to stay in competition, every large commercial bank has to stay abreast of the electronic developments. Inevitably, this has entailed considerable investments in terms of capital and personnel. Huge investments, massive training efforts to inculcate a new management style, and new product development constitute the current highlights of electronic banking.

All this has made strategic planning for electronic banking an area of critical concern for the commercial banks. Not only is the variety of services changing at a rapid pace, but the nature of the technology itself is altering much of the intrinsic character of the banking business.

Naturally, this singular situation has its obvious merits as a topic of research. The fact that there is considerable debate and uncertainty in the industry surrounding the entire subject of converting major segments of operations to the electronic mode also helps in assuring a rich and variegated field for investigation.

However, the emphasis of this study is specifically on individual dynamics rather than the "technical" one conventionally adopted for investigating strategic planning for electronic banking. This focus on the subjective side of strategic planning should help complement the acknowledged effort to improve the technical competence of banking personnel, new ways of information processing, and information use in decision making. In brief, insights into the subjective dynamics of individual strategy makers should benefit both researchers and practitioners in gaining a fuller understanding of the strategy making process.

The book consists of four parts. In Part I, the groundwork is laid for looking at the strategic management process in a subjective-perceptual light, principally by establishing the center-stage role of the strategy maker in that process. Part II discusses the conceptual bases for investigating the individual future orientations of strategy makers and perceived planning milieux. The various research hypotheses of the study are also derived. In Part III, the hypotheses are tested and the findings of the investigation are discussed in detail. Part IV puts forth a number of implications for research as well as the practice of strategy making.

This introductory chapter has laid out the broad boundaries of the investigation, along with a brief outline of the nature of the hypotheses to be examined. The next four chapters set out the theoretical bases for the investigation and the hypotheses.

In Chapter 2, a general framework of the strategy making process is proposed, in which an appropriate emphasis is placed on the critical role of subjective perceptions of all strategy makers. Although not directly relevant to the specific research questions in this study, the chapter attempts to posit a legitimate and realistic role for the subjective side of strategic actors in the strategy making process, thereby balancing to some degree the extant emphasis on an overly rational-analytic conception. Such a preliminary exercise is considered necessary in order to create a reasonable opportunity to complement the current objective-factors research program with a deservedly prominent place for the strategic actors seen as "real person" decision makers embedded in the strategy making process. The chapter thus serves to set the stage for discussing the role of individual future time perspective and perceived planning milieu.

Chapter 3 expatiates on the concept of future time perspective, while Chapter 4 specifically examines the potential relevance of this perspective to the choice of organizational planning horizons. Chapter 5 covers the subject of perception of the internal organizational context of planning, or what has been termed as the planning milieu, and examines the relationship between various kinds of planning milieux and the future time perspective as well as decision making modes.

The research methodology is described in Chapter 6, while Chapter 7 presents some of the demographic characteristics of the executives in the sample. Chapters 8 through 12 contain discussions of the results of the investigation. A replication of the main study with a second sample is discussed in Chapter 13.

Chapters 14 and 15 lay out the conclusions of the study, the managerial implications of the findings, the areas for further research, and some general remarks on a broader agenda for future inquiry.

Finally, it needs to be noted that the overall thrust of this study invites an exploration of diverse literatures. This transdisciplinary perspective precludes a confining attention to the standard corpus of research on strategy making, though that naturally forms the mainstay. It demands a certain intellectual catholicity, along with, unavoidably, the inclusion of referenced material not normally found in discussions of strategy making.

To sum up, the subjective world view of a strategy maker becomes particularly relevant to strategy making in two specific areas: orientation toward the future or "future time perspective," and perception of the internal organizational context of planning or "planning milieu." Both these factors have been ignored in the research literature, and have not been accorded any place in discussions about the practice of strategy making. As a partial attempt to explore the role of these two aspects, this research has examined the relationships (a) between individual future time perspectives of strategy makers and the preference for planning horizons, (b) between individual future time perpectives and the perceived planning milieux, and (c) between the perceptions of the nature of the planning milieux and the decision making modes adopted by organizational members.

In line with the thinking of Homans (1964) to "bring men back in" and of Pondy and Boje (1980) to "bring mind back in," the aim here is to place the individual strategy makers on the center stage of the strategy making enterprise. By doing so, and by placing an adequate emphasis on the subjective elements, it is hoped that we would gain some insights into the dynamics of how individual strategy makers constitute much of the strategy making process through their temporal orientations and perceptions of the strategy making environment.

2
A SUBJECTIVE FRAMEWORK OF
THE STRATEGY MAKING PROCESS

THE SIGNIFICANT ROLE OF STRATEGY MAKER PERCEPTIONS

In its quest for continued survival and growth, a business organization is required to think about future conditions in the environment and how it needs to prepare itself for those conditions. This is usually achieved through strategic planning, which comprises decisions regarding strategic elements over the long run. The adjective "strategic" for the purpose of this investigation "simply means important, in terms of the actions taken, the resources committed, or the precedents set" (Mintzberg, Raisinghani, and Theoret, 1976:246). The manner in which the organization decides to engage itself in strategic planning depends on various factors, of which the individual perceptions of the planning environment by the decision makers is an important one (Anderson and Paine, 1975; Hayes-Roth and Hayes-Roth, 1979; Linder, 1982). The environmental perceptions of the decision makers are important because they serve ultimately to shape the content of the strategic plan. As Anderson and Paine (1975:811-812) put it:

> Depending on perceptions of both environmental and internal properties, managers have considerable leeway in making choices to meet various contingencies ... Strategy formulation is subject to many subjective (behavioral, political, emotional) forces which influence its ultimate form.

This approach does not deny the existence of the objective environment of an organization, but rather complements that notion with another crucial one, namely, that the perceptions of strategic actors have a critical place in the strategy making process. Such a view could be summarized in the words of Bourgeois (1980b:35):

> My position is that the objective task environment is "real," measurable, and external to the organization, and that perceptions of the environment are also real events taking place within the organization. Additionally, and of central importance, when held by the dominant coalition or top management team, these perceptions are considered to be crucial inputs to the strategy-making process.

While researchers have sometimes recognized environmental perceptions of individual strategy makers as having a part in the strategy formulation process, this recognition was not prominently incorporated into the research agenda. There are, however, some emerging signs that a significant role is being posited for these perceptions. Based on their investigation of environmental uncertainty perceptions among 51 division managers of a major U.S. conglomerate, Downey, Hellriegel, and Slocum (1977:172) had the following comments to offer:

> the realization that individual characteristics are related to the manner in which organization members view their environments suggests that physical environmental attributes may not play a "direct" role in determining the internal features of the organization ... Future research should be aimed at exploring the mechanisms by which objective environmental attributes are altered by perceptual processes prior to their influencing internal organization features.

In the specific context of this study, the individual perceptions of organizational members are critical because they affect all stages of the strategy making process, although in different degrees.

A general framework of the strategy making process is developed in this chapter, in which an appropriate emphasis is placed on the critical role of the individual perceptions of all "strategic actors" (who include all organizational

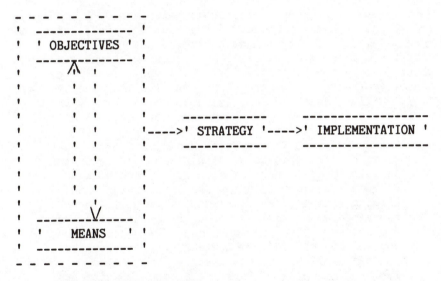

(A) The rational-analytic conception

(B) The political-incremental conception

Figure 2.1: Typical Conceptions of Strategy Making

members engaged in different aspects of the strategy making enterprise). This framework moves away from the traditional rational-analytic model of strategy making, as depicted in part "A" of Figure 2.1 (for representative works, see Andrews, 1980; Ansoff, 1979; Hofer and Schendel, 1978; Steiner, 1969).

The development of strategic management has primarily revolved around the terms environment, objectives, and resources. A certain distancing from this particular historically dominant theme seems warranted in order to attend to the marked lack of the study of behavioral and organizational aspects of strategy making (Cyert and March, 1963). But more pointedly, it is necessary to endow the individual strategy makers (with their unique and differing perceptions) with an appropriately critical role in the research conception of the strategy making process.

The rational decision making theory in classical economic terms is no longer seriously entertained by organizational researchers (Brunsson, 1985; Hogarth, 1980; Janis and Mann, 1977). It is now acknowledged that the reality of decision making is unavoidably a product of bounded rationality, on account of the limited information processing capacity of decision makers (Kahneman, Slovic, and Tversky, 1982; Miller, 1956; Simon, 1976, 1979). March (1981:212) has lucidly explained this abridgement of rational choice:

> Because of such limits, the decision process that is used differs in some significant ways from the decision process anticipated by a more classical formulation. Decision making is seen as problem solving, search, and incremental trial and error. Described as "muddling through" by Lindblom, as "feedback-react" procedures by Cyert and March, and as "cybernetic" by Steinbruner, incremental, limited rationality is usually contrasted with long-run planning, forecasts, and commitments. The intelligence of organizational action is seen as lying not in the capability to know everything in advance but in the ability to make marginal improvements by monitoring problems and searching for solutions. Thus theories of limited rationality are essentially theories of search or attention: What alternatives are considered? What information is used?

In a general sense, the subjective framework could be said to subscribe to the political-incremental school of strategy making, shown in part "B" of Figure 2.1 (as in the works of Bower, 1970; Braybrooke and Lindblom, 1970; Carter, 1971; Chandler, 1962; Lindblom, 1959, 1968, 1979; Murray, 1978; Quinn, 1980; Steinbruner, 1974; Wrapp, 1967). Quinn (1980), in particular, has convincingly integrated the bounded rationality of strategy makers and the strategy making process through his concept of logical incrementalism. The cognitive limitations of the decision maker and the various constraints on the efficiency of the strategic change process make incrementalism the preferred approach:

> top executives typically deal with the logic of
> each subsystem of strategy formulation largely on
> its own merits and usually with a different set of
> people. ...
>
> The most effective strategies of major enterprises
> tend to emerge step by step from an iterative pro-
> cess in which the organization probes the future,
> experiments, and learns from a series of partial
> (incremental) commitments rather than through
> global formulations of total strategies. Good
> managers are aware of this process, and they con-
> sciously intervene in it. Quinn (1980:52,58)

It may be noted that there is also a general stream of integrative approaches in the literature (Camillus, 1982; Donaldson and Lorsch, 1983; Jemison, 1981; Smith and May, 1980).

The framework proposed here could also be seen to bridge, after a fashion, the world of managerial perceptions and behavior with the world of economic-administrative deci- sion making. In whatever way, though, one chooses to inter- pret the dominant themes in the strategy making field, it would appear that individual strategy makers and their per- ceptions in the strategy making process have not been given adequate recognition.

The subjective framework of the strategy making process developed here comprises four segments or stages. These are, respectively, perception of strategy environment, eval- uation of strategy environment, strategy delineation, and strategy implementation (see Figure 2.2). It should be noted that different authorities have suggested different numbers of stages in analyzing the strategy making process. Generally, though, these different schema may be telescoped parsimoniously into the four broad segments proposed here. Obviously, the number of stages being pegged at four is

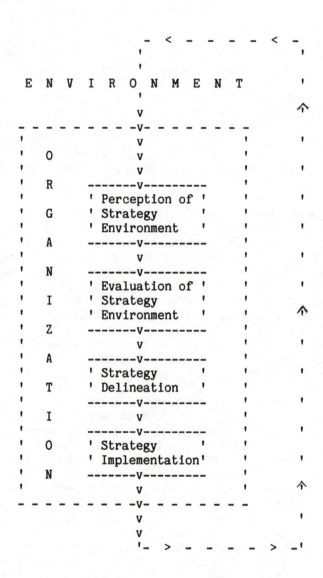

Figure 2.2: Stages of the Strategy Making Process

somewhat arbitrary, as finer or different distinctions can be easily envisaged, including those of goal formulation, alternative generation, and so on (Armstrong, 1982; Greenwood and Thomas, 1981; Steiner, 1969). However, the four stages are considered a reasonable compromise in the interest of avoiding an inordinately complex classification.

A SUBJECTIVE FRAMEWORK

The first of the four stages in the framework -- the perception of the strategy environment by the strategy maker -- is a highly individualistic one, so that there is considerable scope for differences among the strategy makers as to the "correct" interpretation of environmental characteristics. The importance of this initial stage in the process is largely dissipated today in a debate over whether the organizational environment which is relevant to researchers is "objective" or "perceived," and the attendant difficulties of measuring the relative phenomena (Smircich and Stubbart, 1985). The part played by the individual strategic actors is often lost sight of. Individuals behave in relation to the personal universes and world pictures that they construct (Harrison, 1985). It needs to be reiterated that it is the interpretations of the individual organizational participants that ultimately lead to organizational responses. As Daft and Weick (1984:293) have explained:

> one of the widely held tenets in organizational theory is that the external environment will influence organization structure and design ... But that relationship can be manifested only if participants within the organization sense and interpret the environment and respond to it. Almost all outcomes in terms of organization structure and design, whether caused by the environment, technology, or size, depend on the interpretation of problems or opportunities by key decision makers.

The vital role that the first (perceptual) stage may have in "conditioning" the later stages, is a subject deserving serious attention. Also, as will be argued later, as one moves through its four stages, the process exhibits a discrete shift from a predominance of the perceptual mode to a relatively more analytical approach, and then back to an emphasis on the perceptual factor.

The process of strategy making, as depicted in Figure 2.2, does not view the strategy content as an end-product. Rather, the outcomes of implementation of the strategy are recursively looped to a subsequent round of perception of the consequentially "molded environment." The entire process is thus cyclical and reflexive in nature (Schulman, 1976), with each cycle progressing along a spiral of interacting individual perceptions, strategic actions, and environmental reactions. The model incorporates the crucial, but often neglected, perceptual-cognitive aspect in the conventionally rational perspective of organizational decision making. While the initial stage in the model is predominantly of a perceptual nature, the subsequent two stages have an increasingly analytic content.

PERCEPTION OF STRATEGY ENVIRONMENT

Graham (1968:292) points out that "an individual's reaction within a situation is a function of his perception of the situation rather than his interaction with a solitary combination of 'real' stimuli and constraints." Edward de Bono has observed that

> there is no such thing as neutral objective information in the mind. For example, the word "textile" spoken to a group will mean his wife's dress to one executive, a low profit area to another, Japanese competition to a third, labor troubles to a fourth. In each case, the concept of "textile" is embedded in a personal pattern of experience. Even though it may seem possible to extract an abstract neutral concept of "textiles" this requires deliberate effort and is never really neutral (quoted in Heirs and Pehrson, 1977:7).

Depending, then, upon the way the environment is perceived by different individuals, there would be differing responses. These perceptions are importantly associated with the degree of uncertainty in the environment.

An attempt at clarifying the perceptual view of environmental uncertainty was made by Duncan (1972), who related the perceived uncertainty experienced by managers to two dimensions of the environment, namely, complexity and dynamism. Environmental uncertainty was measured by (a) lack of information regarding the environmental factors associated with a given situation, (b) not knowing the outcome of a specific decision in terms of how much the organization would lose if the decision were incorrect, and (c) inability to assign probabilities with any degree of confidence with regard to how environmental factors are going to affect the success or failure of the decision unit in performing its function. The study found that the least perceived uncertainty was associated with simple-static environments, while the highest perceived uncertainty was reported in complex-dynamic environments. Based on his research, Duncan (1972:325) states that the characteristics of organizational environments are variable, since these are "dependent on the perceptions of organization members and thus can vary in their incidence to the extent that individuals differ in their perceptions."

Not surprisingly, therefore, it has been found that the manner in which the environment is dealt with is influenced by the perceptions of the organizational decision makers (McCaskey, 1976). In their study of top executive decision making in a dozen leading corporations, Donaldson and Lorsch (1983:79) observed: "Among the corporate managers in each of the companies we found a distinctive system of beliefs. These interrelated beliefs act as a filter through which management perceives the realities facing its firm."

In studying the impact of environmental factors on behavior in organizations, Dill (1958:443) recognized the role of individual cognition, and concluded that organizational studies "should put explicit emphasis on the cognitive activities of organizational participants as a link between environmental 'stimuli' and the participants' overt 'responses.'" Commenting on the information perspective relating to organizational environments, Aldrich (1979:132) has rightly identified the central role of perceptions of organization members:

> The view of environments as information directs our attention immediately to the role of perception. It posits a two-step flow, with information about environmental elements passing through the filtering out of equivocality, and the filtered information then integrated into the frame of reference of decision makers. The resource view of environments has not really confronted the issue of cognition and perception, either treating the flow of "correct" information as nonproblematic or as irrelevant for explaining how environments affect organizational change. Situations may arise in which a resource is not critical for an

organization's survival, but decision makers view it as crucial and act on their definition of the situation. A number of studies have shown how organizations can create and act on myths and collective symbols (Clark, 1972). Such situations can only be discovered if an investigator is alert to the possibility of selective perception and information processing.

Hence, the perceptions of strategy makers are a significant element in the way the organization goes about constructing a strategy (Neisser, 1976).

There is also another kind of perceptual impact, in which the decision maker "manufactures" a degree of certainty in the otherwise uncertain and amorphous organizational environment. This is done through "structuring" the environment in a manner which builds or organizes (reorganizes?) certainty in it. As Chamberlain (1968:34) put it:

Throughout recorded history individuals -- not only businessmen -- have often grasped at devices which will give them faith in a particular future, and thus replace in their own minds uncertainty with certainty, whatever others may think.

From a somewhat different perspective, Weick (1979) has proposed that environments are enacted or generated by the organization through selective attention to certain environmental elements. The fact is that given the limited capacity of an individual strategy maker, it would be unrealistic to expect a thorough scrutiny of all possible explanations for the myriad bits of information being received (March and Simon, 1958). Hence existing beliefs about the nature of the environment tend to act as a sieve to render the relentlessly accumulating information more humanly manageable. The strategy maker, in effect, "sees what he believes" about the environment (Weick, 1979). "Consequently, a perceiver's ability to organize and interpret his observations depends very strongly on the theories and beliefs he holds a priori, and he tends to learn what he already believed" (Starbuck, 1976:1080).

In terms of cognitive theory, a decision maker, in his or her mind, so fashions the outcomes of alternative courses of actions that the preferred alternative seems favorable. Information processing biases, the employment of heuristic procedures, and cognitive strain are known to delimit optimal decision making choices (MacCrimmon and Taylor, 1976;

Schwenk, 1985; Wright, 1980). People oftentimes have perceptions of outcomes of events unconsciously or semicons-
ciously influenced by their hopes, wishes, and expectations
(Cyert, Dill, and March, 1958).

All strategic plans are in any event partly constituted
by hopes, beliefs, and myths (Broms and Gahmberg, 1983). A
false feeling of control over an uncertain future is often
engendered merely on account of dealing with uncertain event
outcomes (Langer, 1975), and there is a tendency to credit
one's skills for success and to attribute failure to chance
and bad luck (Miller, 1976). Corporate failures could
result from a reluctance to accept available facts and the
prevalence of bounded-vision among dominant decision makers
(Huxham and Dando, 1981). Also, some uncertainties are simply ignored or discounted in order to arrive at a best-guess
alternative. As Steinbruner (1974:123) explains:

> Under complexity, the mind, in this view, does not
> match the uncertain structure of the environment
> in which events might take a number of alternative
> courses. Rather, it imposes an image and works to
> preserve that image.

The process by which this selection of a single preferred outcome is achieved is by selective attention to
incoming information. "The cybernetic decision maker is
sensitive to information only if it enters through an estab-
lished highly focused feedback channel, and hence many factors which do in fact affect the outcomes have no effect in
his decision process" (Steinbruner, 1974:67). In relation
to organizations, the analysis of Cohen, March, and Olsen
(1976:32) provides a similar explanation:

> Since an organization can attend to only a limited
> part of available information, attempts are made
> to invent mechanisms for increasing sensitivity to
> some kinds of information and insensitivity to
> others. Organizational mechanisms are developed
> for ascribing meaning, relevance, and priority to
> different types of inputs.

The selective allocation of attention to specific
information, or specific elements of the organizational
environment, is mostly of a normative character and is often
subjectively irrational. More attention tends to be allocated to tasks which are immediate and which can be accomplished conveniently. Also, not unsurprisingly, "the

distribution of attention ... depended on what higher management noticed" (Stinchcombe, 1974:24). And, "some things
rarely receive attention unless there is nothing else to do
... (such as) long-run planning, thinking, nonfamiliar
problems and ambiguous objectives" (March and Olsen,
1976:50). The strategic decision maker has bounded rationality, a restricted field of vision, perceives a situation
on a selective basis, and interprets the selected bits of
information through a filter (Daft and Weick, 1984).

It needs to be noted also that strategic problems are,
almost by definition, ill-structured and "messy," and demand
design and synthesizing skills based on intellectual abili-
ties which are qualitatively different from those required
for operational problems (Ackoff, 1981; McMillan, 1980;
Mintzberg, Raisinghani, and Theoret, 1976; Simon, 1970,
1973). Top level decision making, according to a government
executive, is usually nonlogarithmic, creative, free-form,
open-loop, and personal (Borsting, 1982:350).

In sum, it could be said that there would be differential responses among individual strategy makers according as
how the strategy environment is perceived by them, and the
amount of attention allocated to various aspects of that
environment. This has been explained by Vickers (1965) in
terms of what he calls "appreciative judgments." These
judgments "reflect the view currently held by those who made
them of their interests and responsibilities, views largely
implicit and unconscious which none the less condition what
events and relations they will regard as relevant or possi-
bly relevant to them, and whether they will regard these as
welcome or unwelcome, important or unimportant, demanding or
not demanding action or concern by them" (Vickers, 1965:67).
Thus the same environment may be perceived as more or less
stable or uncertain or competitive by different strategy
makers, contingent perhaps on how they are positioned and
what their activities are. It would thus seem reasonable to
go beyond the so-called objective measures of the strategy
environment, and to recognize the critical part played by
the perceptions of the strategy makers.

EVALUATION OF STRATEGY ENVIRONMENT

Emery and Trist (1965) are credited with pointing out
that the environment can be visualized as being made up of
one or more of four ideal types, depending upon the extent
of interrelationships of its various components and the rate
of change. They designated the four types as placid-random-

ized, placid-clustered, disturbed-reactive, and turbulent. In the case of the turbulent environment, there is considerable complexity and accelerated change -- easily identified as the one typically faced by many modern business organizations. The heterogeneity of the environment has no doubt led to some thinking about environmental uncertainty. Uncertainty has been viewed by some researchers as synonymous with rapid environmental change (Lawrence and Lorsch, 1967). Thompson (1967) treats the two features of heterogeneity and dynamism (or change) quite separately, while Duncan (1972), as noted earlier, combines them to derive the concept of uncertainty.

The various elements in the environment are usually evaluated against the backdrop of corporate intentions and capabilities, as a necessary step -- this with a clear constriction of the perceptual mode, with a corresponding expansion of the analytic element -- for generating alternative strategic actions to comprise a strategic plan. Environmental scanning activities have been investigated comprehensively by researchers. The focus has been, not surprisingly, on the objective factors (Aguilar, 1967; Lenz and Engledow, 1986; Utterback, 1979). Recently, though, Daft and Weick (1984) have proposed a model which accommodates the subjective factor by suggesting that organizations can be seen as interpretive systems in terms of Boulding's scale of system complexity (Boulding, 1956).

Without going into that model, one can easily discern from a reading of the four stages of environmental scanning suggested by Aguilar (1967:19-21) how the environmental perception progressively becomes an analytical activity, with a gradually reduced role for subjective perceptions. The four stages are:

1. "Undirected viewing" -- general exposure to information with no specific purpose in mind ... (and) general unawareness as to what issues might be raised. ... involves a considerable degree of orientation on the part of the scanner by virtue of his selection of particular sources and his general experience and interest.

2. "Conditioned viewing" -- directed exposure, not involving active search, to a more or less identified area or type of information ... (but) the viewer is sensitive to particular kinds of data and is ready to assess their significance.

3. "Informal search" -- relatively limited and unstructured effort to obtain specific information or information for a specific purpose.

4. "Formal search" -- deliberate effort -- usually following a pre-established plan, procedure, or methodology -- to secure specific information or
information relating to a specific issue.

The formal, analytical content of the scanning exercise
steadily increases in the later stages, leaving progressively less room for individual idiosyncratic evaluations.

After evaluating its environment, the organization has
to select a specific slice or area in which it will operate.
The area it chooses to operate in, or its domain, will of
course be a part of the task environment of the organization. The task environment is composed of those elements of
the environment which are relevant or potentially relevant
to the goal setting and attainment of the organization.
Only a portion of this task environment is chosen by the
organization as its operational field, and this particular
part of the environment would be the domain of the organization (Levine and White, 1961).

The selection of the domain would be based upon the
kinds of inputs (technology, materials, services) and out-
puts (products, services, etc.) that are involved. The
resources that are being exchanged between the organization
and the environment can be best defined as "the generalized
means, or facilities, that are potentially controllable by
social organizations, and that are potentially usable --
however indirectly -- in relationships between the organization and its environment" (Yuchtman and Seashore, 1967:900).
The proper selection of the domain is crucial because the
ability to acquire adequate resources from the environment,
in order to be able to take desired strategic actions, would
depend on the nature of the domain selected (Meyer, 1975).

Much of the content of strategic actions would thus
seem to depend on the subjective evaluation of the environment and the associated selection of the domain. The role
of the strategy maker as an individual with limited capacity
and satisficing tendency continues to be prominent. There
would be no point in assuming that all the crucial variables
would be identified for assessing the opportunities and
threats in the environment, and indeed that would be impos-
sible.

STRATEGY DELINEATION

The evaluation of the environment constitutes the preparation for a strategic plan -- which is the tangible culmi-
nation of an organization's efforts to deal with the
environment. Organizations are rarely passive agents
absorbing environmental pressures. Child (1972) has argued
that organizations attempt to manipulate environmental features through strategic actions. Organizations also enact
their own environment (Weick, 1979) and try to exercise control over it.

In its effort to have some influence over its environment, every organization adopts certain measures or strategies, which collectively hang from the peg of the strategic
plan. It has been observed that as changes take place in
the environment (in taste, products, technologies), the for-
tunes of a firm change with it. Anticipating the future,
and preparing for it, thus becomes the central concern of a
firm. Chamberlain (1968:202-203) has captured this thrust
of strategy making in the following words:

> (The firm) must therefore try to anticipate the
> future and its own state of readiness for it. If
> it is to maintain the value of its assets, it must
> redeploy them in forms appropriate for a changed
> set of circumstances, but changed in ways not
> wholly predictable. Hence the effort to control
> -- to create -- what it cannot predict.

Chandler (1962:13-14), who studied American industrial
enterprise at some length, defines strategy in terms plainly
recognizing the active role of organization members:

> Strategy can be defined as the determination of
> the basic long-term goals and objectives of an
> enterprise, and the adoption of courses of action
> and the allocation of resources necessary for car-
> rying out these goals. Decisions to expand the
> volume of activities, to set up distant plants and
> offices, to move into new economic functions, or
> become diversified along many lines of business,
> involve the defining of new basic goals. New
> courses of action must be devised and resources
> allocated and reallocated in order to achieve
> these goals and to maintain and expand the firm's
> activities in the new areas in response to shift-
> ing demands, changing sources of supply, fluctuat-

ing economic conditions, new technological developments, and the actions of competitors. As the adoption of a new strategy may add new types of personnel and facilities, and alter the business horizons of the men responsible for the enterprise, it can have a profound effect on the form of its organization.

In all the areas alluded to in the definition, the intention of the strategy makers to act upon the environment is clear. Following Weick's (1979) concept of enactment, Pondy and Mitroff (1979:13) have observed that "one of an organization's most crucial design decisions concern how it attempts to design its own environment."

Several of the ways in which organizations manage their environments have been documented by various researchers (Aldrich, 1979; Pfeffer and Salancik, 1978). Briefly, these are through mergers, joint ventures, movement of personnel between organizations, and cooptation and interlocking boards of directors, subject of course to the firm's strategic capabilities. The object of these methods of intervening in the environment is to modify the turbulence that Emery and Trist talked about, into something which we might term as "structured turbulence." That, in brief, is the object of delineation of a strategy.

The mechanics of strategy delineation need not concern us here, except to note that the perceptual mode yields in a large measure to the analytical. But even here, it may be mentioned, a more realistic understanding of the process could result if one takes into account the values and systematic judgment biases of individual strategy makers (Larwood and Whittaker, 1977; Lyles and Mitroff, 1985; For instance, Bazerman and Schoorman (1983) have proposed a multilevel, limited rationality model of interlocking directorates, in which the subjective viewpoints of the participating directors are incorporated along with organizational and societal perspectives.

It is often one thing to develop a good strategic plan and quite another to have it implemented by the operating people in the proper spirit. The difficulty arises primarily out of the misplaced confidence of strategy makers that their technical expertise is sufficient for making good strategic decisions. They tend to forget that the rational approach to organizational decision making is at best an incomplete one, if only because our knowledge of any problem situation is restricted to the content part only. As the illustration given below demonstrates, even in the case of a fairly ordinary situation, a solution based purely upon rational methods may fail to take into account certain otherwise important factors.

The problem of determining the minimum number of tellers in a commercial bank branch necessary to just meet the needs of customers is a classic one. It is necessary to judge the trade-off point between the cost of idle time if the number of tellers is too many, and the extent of inconvenience caused to the waiting customers if this number is too few. Churchman (1968:24-25) makes the following interesting observations to indicate the inadequacies of a rational approach:

> an idle teller need not be idle while waiting at a station where there are no customers. Instead he may be occupied with other routine matters requiring attention in the administration of the bank. Consequently, if the manager can design the entire operation of his bank's many functions properly, he may be able to decrease the cost of idle time of personnel who are servicing customers. If we look on the other side of the picture, i.e., the inconvenience to a customer, we may find that in fact waiting in line is not an inconvenience at all if the customer happens to meet an acquaintance there. Perhaps the manager should serve coffee and doughnuts to waiting customers. ... in many cases banks set up Express Windows to handle customers who would normally have very low service times. Hence, an overall average waiting time may not make sense if there are different types of services tailored to the various needs of the customers.

All this just goes to show that an over-emphasis on rationality may actually hinder effectiveness. This is particularly important as it is the human agency which ultimately operates a scheme or gives an idea a practical shape in the real world of activity; also, it is the human agency which bears the cost of change, in a far more direct manner than the strategy makers themselves.

STRATEGY IMPLEMENTATION

The implementation aspect of strategy making, in the form usually of strategic planning, has rightly been receiving increasing attention in recent years (see, for example, Bourgeois and Brodwin, 1984; Hrebiniak and Joyce, 1984; Lorange, 1982; MacMillan and Guth, 1985). However, most of the attention seems to be concentrated on the implementation of strategies or formal strategic planning systems as whole entities. The focus in the present exposition, however, is not on the implementation of planning systems, but rather on the implementation phase of the strategic planning process (analytically subsequent to the delineation of a plan). The activities in this phase imply that strategy makers can and do make an impact on the task environment.

Clearly, it would not be possible for an organization to completely condition or shape the task environment according to its desire. However, what is more to the point is that by being able to at least partially fashion the environment, an organization can have more options in terms of applicable alternative strategies (Thompson and McEwen, 1958; Child, 1972). The activity of strategic planning, driven and conditioned by individual perceptions of the planning environment, is evidence that organizations are in no way helpless entities in a capriciously turbulent environment.

While the rational-analytic mode still has an important part in this last stage of strategy implementation, the role of individual perceptions once again assume a certain amount of dominance. This is because there is less relevance for the formal rules and procedures in the substantially discretionary field of actually going about implementing or achieving the planned strategic goals. As Weick and Daft (1983:90-91) put it, "the job of management is to interpret, not to get the work of the organization done." In terms of the process of strategy making, the implementation stage can be described as largely subjective in its overall character.

A neglected aspect of implementation of strategic planning has to do with the subjective understanding of the planning process as well as the plan by the strategy makers. This "understanding" is in addition to the mere "acceptance" of the plan, and neither of these factors has received adequate attention in the literature on strategy implementation. Here, as in other areas, cognitive styles of the strategic actors become salient (McKenney and Keen, 1974).

There are umpteen examples in business and industry where strategic plans have failed to yield expected results, not because of any technical fault or inadequacy, but because incorrect assumptions were made about organizational behavior while carrying out the relative investigations. Nevertheless, the belief persists, despite protestations to the contrary, that everything is done rationally in an organization.

Implementation has two principal aspects. One, which needs no discussion here, is that the plans have to be feasible and applicable to the real-life situation. In other words, they have to be practical and have obvious advantages in terms of organizational productivity and growth. The other aspect is that of acceptance and understanding by the strategy makers. No change can be brought about without this crucial element of acceptance. Also, if acceptance is not coupled with an understanding (Lorange, 1982:9), implementation would suffer from possible organizational instabilities.

DIFFERENTIAL IMPACT OF SUBJECTIVE PERCEPTIONS

The four stages in the strategy making process, illustrated in Figure 2.2, have been described in terms of their conceptual bases. The factor which is crucial in understanding the strategy making process is the role of perceptions. The concept of perceived environmental uncertainty, especially, is central to the entire process, as it affects the initial perception of environmental characteristics by the strategy makers.

Environmental uncertainty, for instance, is gradually reduced through perceptual "structuring." There is a gradual increase in the degree of certainty concerning the strategy environment -- artificially contrived through individual perception, as has been maintained here -- as the information processing proceeds from perception onwards to evaluation and subsequent stages. This escalation of proportionate analytic content (and accompanying certainty) has been represented diagrammatically in Figure 2.3. The second and third stages in the subjective framework (Figure 2.2), it should be noted, are influenced in varying degrees by the (internal) operating procedures of the organization, an environment which tends to be more regulated and orderly (hence more predictable and certain) than the external organizational environment.

The first stage in the strategy making process -- the perception of the strategy environment -- is a highly individualistic one, giving rise to differences among strategy makers as to the proper assessment of environmental characteristics. While the subsequent three stages of the process have been the subject of much investigation, the part played by the first (perceptual) stage is significant in "condi-

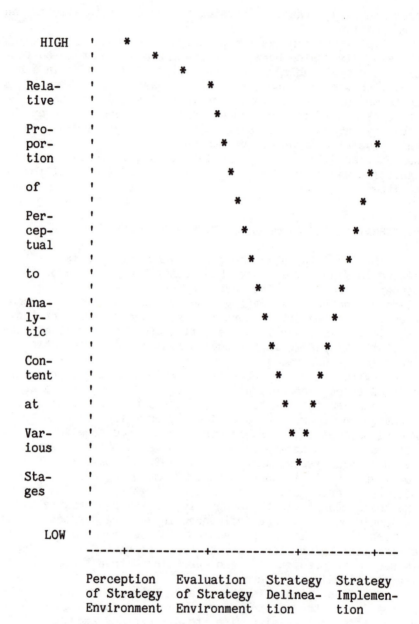

Figure 2.3: Perceptual-Analytic Content in Strategy Making

tioning" the later stages. It is hoped that researchers in the area of business strategy will find the process model presented here useful in designing their investigations about the strategy making enterprise.

Concisely, then, strategy making may be defined as the behavior of the organization toward the environment. This (strategic) behavior is largely determined by the strategy makers of the organization. The object of the planned strategic actions is to "structure a new environment which will be favorable to it" (Chamberlain, 1968:203). All such actions, however, are influenced by the environmental perceptions activated originally by the agency of individual strategy makers. That these perceptions are modified iteratively and reflexively (Schulman, 1976), as the process of strategy making cycles over time, does not in any way detract from the above basic contention. The original perceptions are of course modified subsequently by increasingly-analytic processes of evaluation of the environment and strategy delineation. To use a different metaphor, planned strategic actions are intrinsically the creatures of environmental perceptions of the strategy makers. Borrowing from Marshall McLuhan's famous statement that "the medium is the message," one could say here with reason that "perceptions are the strategy" and "perceptions are the plan."

PART II
FUTURE ORIENTATIONS AND PLANNING MILIEUX

3

FUTURE ORIENTATIONS
OF STRATEGY MAKERS

RELEVANCE OF RESEARCH ON TIME IN OTHER DISCIPLINES

Research on individual time perspective can be found in various disciplines, but very little of this can be related directly to business, especially in the area of strategy making. That individuals experience the passage of time differentially is amply demonstrated both in everyday life and in the literature. Indeed, the subjective experience of a time perspective is a common notion in various disciplines.

A general discussion of the concept of time or the future time dimension is clearly beyond the scope of this investigation. It should be noted, though, that a fairly substantial literature exists on the subject of time in various disciplines, most notably in philosophy, physics, psychology, anthropology, history, and sociology (Das, in process).

Strategy makers and researchers interested in the subject of time would do well to start with some items from the the following eclectic list of general surveys, commentaries, essay collections, and theoretical expositions: Carlstein, Parkes, and Thrift (1978), Doob (1971), Fraser (1981), Fraser, Haber, and Muller (1972), Fraser and Lawrence (1975), Fraser, Lawrence, and Park (1978), Fraser, Park, and Lawrence (1981), Gale (1968a), Gorman and Wessman (1977), Greenaway (1979), Gurvitch (1964), Hall (1983), Michon and Jackson (1985), Morris (1984), Orme (1969), Ornstein (1970), Sherover (1975), Toulmin and Goodfield (1982), Whitrow (1980), and Yaker, Osmond, and Cheek (1972).

The literature on time contains a plethora of theories and speculations. The interested reader may consult some of the following for a glimpse of the variety: Brumbaugh (1984), Denbigh (1981), Dunne (1927), Fraser (1978), Gale (1968b), Husserl (1964), McTaggart (1968), Mellor (1981), Newton-Smith (1980), and Reichenbach (1971).

As an indication of the kind of theorizing that awaits the student of time, we mention the intriguing thesis of a two-dimensional concept of time compatible with a world view of a five-dimensional space-time manifold, which has recently been proposed by Elliott Jaques, a researcher in the business field. He explains the two dimensions as follows:

> The first dimension is the temporal axis of intention, the time by which we intend, or plan, or seek to accomplish something; and the second dimension is the temporal axis of succession, the axis along which we standardize our calendars and clocks. ...
>
> Our ideas of past, present, and future, passage and direction, flux and change, duree and continuity, are exclusively associated with the temporal axis of intention. They are expressions of our field experience in the flowing present. The past is the flow of memory, the present of perception, and the future of expectation and desire. ...
>
> Our ideas of earlier and later, before and after, temporal discontinuity and atomism, constancy and permanence are, by contrast, exclusively associated with the temporal axis of succession. They are expressions of our experience of a cross-sectional or spatial abstraction from events, ...
>
> In terms of time, it takes us to the notion of continual cognitive oscillation between intention and succession, between past, present, and future and earlier and later, ... (Jaques, 1982:xii-xiii)

One is constrained to remark, though, that while the literature on time in various disciplines is considerable and fascinating per se, the relevance of most of the thinking, save some parts of psychology, to the field of business in general and of strategy making in particular is at best somewhat tenuous.

RESEARCH ON TIME IN THE BUSINESS AREA

It should be noted, nevertheless, that there is some evidence of the time factor being considered by business scholars in recent years, albeit in a halting and sporadic manner. Traditionally, the subject of time has been dealt with only in terms of the efficient use of a physical resource, as in problems of time allocation, time management, time and motion studies, time budgeting, and so forth. A quite different stream of inquiry employed the time-span of discretion as a measure of the level of responsibility in a job situation (Hill, 1956; Jaques, 1956, 1964, 1979). The time horizon of work is another example of using the time dimension in studying the differentiation and integration mechanisms in organizations for tasks with varying degrees of uncertainty (Lawrence and Lorsch, 1967).

A logical place to look for research concerning the future time dimension would seem to be the growing field of futures research (Cornish et al, 1977; Fowles, 1978; Linstone and Simmonds, 1977). Surprisingly, though, the future time dimension does not appear to be treated in the least as problematic (see, for example, Amara, 1978; Bell and Mau, 1971; Huber, 1978; Morrison, Renfro, and Boucher, 1983).

The few publications that deal with the role of futures studies in strategy making have not addressed the psychological dimension of future time, confining the discussion strictly to the conventional mold of forecasting, scenario building, and so on (Ascher and Overholt, 1983; Becker, 1985; Edmunds, 1982; Evered, 1973; Fildes and Wood, 1978; Helmer, 1979; Holloway, 1978; Leemhuis, 1985; Malaska, 1985; Wack, 1985; Zentner, 1982). The future dimension is also implicitly the backdrop of forecasting, but here too the approach is mostly guided by extrapolatory techniques, with little accommodation of human temporal judgments (Bunge, 1973; Cole, 1977; de Jouvenel, 1967; Encel, Marstrand, and Page, 1975; Gordon and Stover, 1976; Hogarth and Makridakis, 1981; Makridakis and Wheelwright, 1981; Naylor, 1983).

In the last decade or so, there have been some tentative efforts to study the relevance of the temporal dimension to organizational behavior and business topics -- see, for instance, Cummings (1982), El Sawy (1983), Graham (1981), Jacoby, Szybillo, and Berning (1976), Katz (1980), and McGrath and Rotchford (1983). Jacoby et al (1976) discuss the relationship between time and consumer behavior as reflected in the literature of economics, sociology, home economics, psychology, and marketing. Graham (1981) examines the more fundamental issue of how extant consumer behavior models are intrinsically predicated upon a specific way of perceiving time, namely, as essentially linear in nature, with discretely separable units of past, present, and future. He contends that this underlying assumption regarding time perception gives rise to inadequacies in the present consumer behavior models when applied to individuals who have a different perception of time, such as what he terms as circular-traditional and procedural-temporal.

The paper by Katz (1980) develops a framework describing how each job tenure period attracts a different set of common issues and concerns on the part of employees. The notion of time employed is merely one of how long an individual has been in a job situation. Cummings (1982:566-567) takes note of some of the recent research which incorporates the passage of time as a variable in organizational behavior.

The review by McGrath and Rotchford (1983) covers some of the dominant conceptions of time as found in philosophy, physics, biology, and psychology. They suggest that time as a biological phenomenon and as a subjective phenomenon may affect individual behavior in organizations. They also apply the notion of time as a cultural phenomenon to discuss temporal issues in organizations.

The study by El Sawy (1983) is one which begins to address business concerns in an explicit manner. The chief executive officers of 37 high technology companies formed the sample. The companies were small to medium in size. The study investigated the relationships between the temporal perspectives of the executives and various phases of the strategic attention process. The perception of how personal events were placed in time constituted the temporal perspective of an individual executive. The manner in which the executives searched for opportunities and threats in the external environments of the companies was the basis for determining strategic attention. It was found that the two factors, temporal perspective and strategic attention, had significant associations. As an illustration of the kind of linkages that the study revealed, the executives with longer future horizons seemed to utilize more impersonal sources of strategic information (such as trade journals, conferences, etc.) in contrast with those having shorter future horizons.

These endeavors are admittedly desultory in its overall thrust, but it seems to be a happy development if one subscribes to the view that the influence of time in business and organizational affairs needs to be examined at a more sophisticated level than in the past (Clark, 1978). The critical point to note, though, is that in none of the works cited above, except that of El Sawy (1983) in some measure, is there any discussion of the notion of future time perspective in the sense that seems most relevant in strategy making. It is to this task that the rest of this chapter is devoted.

CONCEPT OF FUTURE TIME PERSPECTIVE

As a point of departure for appreciating the relevance of the time dimension in strategic management (and business studies in general), a case could be made for sensitizing oneself to the multi-faceted splendor of the time construct through a reading of some of the literature in various disciplines. For this investigation, we intend to borrow some gleanings from psychology that relate especially to the conception of the future time perspective. Our interest lies in the subjective perceptions of individuals about the future time dimension, and not in the objective clock or calendar time.

Definitions of time perspective are generally based on the notion of an individual having an inner life-space within which all events have been ordered in a meaningful way. Wallace and Rabin (1960:213) have stated that it "revolves around the relationships between persons' past, present and future within their phenomenal frames of reference." Lewin (1951:75) has defined time perspective as "the totality of an individual's views of his psychological past and psychological future existing at a given time."

It should be noted parenthetically that the discussion here is not concerned with the main body of work on time in the field of psychology, namely, time perception. That work has to do principally with knowledge about the duration estimation of the passage of time (Cohen, 1954; Cottle, 1969; Fraisse, 1981, 1984). Nor is this investigation concerned with mental imageries of one's personal future (Boulding, 1961), or grand scenarios for the future of institutions, societies, and the world (Ackoff, 1974; Ayres, 1979; Emery and Trist, 1973; Forrester, 1961, 1971; Jones, 1980; Kahn and Wiener, 1967; Meadows, Meadows, Randers, and Behrens, 1972; Polak, 1973), or various prognostications of trends in the future (Bell, 1973; Bundy, 1976; Gribbin, 1981; McHale, 1969; Muller, 1974; Naisbitt, 1982; Toffler, 1971, 1981), or the potpourri of analyses about future thinking (Dean, Mihalasky, Ostrander, and Schroder, 1974;

Loye, 1978). All these facets of the subject of the future, some quite attractive in the popular mind, have very little relevance to the notion of individual future time perspective that is of interest here.

The rationale for studying time perspective, especially that relating to the future, has been indicated by Cohen (1981:262) in the following words: "A subjective future is supposed in all our activities. ... Implicit in all our actions are plans, however vague and inarticulate, for the future, and sometimes, as in saving and investment, this planning is deliberate." A similar justification is advanced by Kelly (1958:59):

> Always the future beckons him and always he reaches out in tremulous anticipation to touch it. He lives in anticipation; ... His behavior is governed, not simply by what he anticipates -- whether good or bad, pleasant or unpleasant, self-vindicating or self-confounding -- but by where he believes his choices will place him in respect to the remaining turns in the road.

According to Fraisse (1963:173), there are basically two ways an individual can look at the future -- either as "the prospect of a conquest toward which we are advancing," or as "the anticipation of something indeterminate." One may stress one or the other mode, depending on whether one adopts a passive or a proactive stance. Either way, though, the anticipation of the time yet to come about would play a dominant role in the formation of an individual's time perspective (Thomae, 1981). Fraisse (1963:176) explains:

> The future perspectives of an individual depend, then, on his capacity for anticipating what is to come. This anticipation is a form of construction determined by the individual. It borrows from his past experience, but it is prompted by his present desires and fits into the framework of what he considers to belong to the realm of possibility... This control over time is essentially an individual achievement conditioned by everything which determines personality: age, environment, temperament, experience. Each individual has his own perspective.

People also have a tendency to place a lower value to happenings in the future in relation to the present.

According to Linstone (1973, 1977), some of the ineffectiveness of long range planning can be explained by the pervasive tendency to discount the future. He says that people

> apply a psychological discount rate to our perception of future problems and opportunities the same way a businessman applies a discount rate to future income ... An oil shortage thirty years from now is not perecived nearly as serious a crisis as the same shortage occurring in six months. We look at the future as if through the wrong end of a telescope." (Linstone, 1977:5)

This phenomenon of discounting of the future is often made worse by the unwitting reinforcement provided by researchers. Adelson and Aroni (1975:436) have commented that in studies relating to the preferences and values of people, researchers are prone to present respondents with alternatives that are inherently rooted in the present:

> Alternatives explored in such studies tend to be those which are practical today. The more distant futures, with its more diverse set of alternatives, is deemphasized. Interest centers on micro-decisions. Images of the present, based more often than not on limited experience of the past, tend to be accepted as images of the future. The limitations of such images may exert a constraining effect on what possibilities the future can contain.

It is apparent that the stranglehold of the present can serve to effectively suffocate much of the potential life of the future. There is some reason to ponder over the past too to improve business decision making (Neustadt and May, 1986).

RESEARCH RELATING TO FUTURE TIME PERSPECTIVE

While a large number of psychological studies deal with pathological subjects, there is a small body of research regarding the healthy personality that is of some interest to the business world. However, the studies have rarely been carried out with subjects in the business world. Some illustrative findings are mentioned here to provide a flavor of the research thrust in the literature.

Lessing (1968:199-200), for instance, found that in cases where significant relationships existed between the length of future time perspective (FTP) and other variables, "the longer FTP was always associated with more favorable psychological attributes (e.g., higher intelligence, higher academic achievement, higher socioeconomic status and healthier personality test scores)." In regard to the preference for delayed reward and future time perspective, Klineberg (1968:256) has noted that "the capacity to choose a larger reward, delayed for a short and specified period of time, over a smaller reward available immediately is related to the degree to which personal future events in general appear to be endowed with a sense of reality, as well as to the degree of everyday preoccupation with future rather than present events." Similarly, de Volder and Lens (1982) report that a significantly higher valence to goals in the distant future is attached by students with higher grade point average and higher study persistence compared to other students with lower scores. Other investigations have dealt with the relationship between future time perspective and other variables, such as learning and motivation (Nuttin, 1964).

In one of the earlier contributions, Kastenbaum (1961) explored a four-variable model of future time perspective using a group of high school students. Based upon his study, Kastenbaum (1961:215-216) suggested a research agenda which in some fashion advances a broad rationale for the present investigation:

> there is much that could be accomplished ... by exploring the interrelationships between future time perspective and certain other temporal variables.
>
> The study of planning abilities, for example, seems closely related to future outlook. Both sets of variables show definite reference to the future, the planning process having more obvious connection to the individual's choice of behavior and purposive manipulation of the environment. FTP might be regarded as that function of the individual which permits him to draw up a model of the future, while planning refers to his process of working within that self-defined framework. A joint investigation of FTP and planning ability might make it possible to reformulate both the concepts in a broader manner, avoiding the arbitrary restrictions that have thus far kept these two bodies of research apart.

In this study, the strategy makers are classified in terms of their individual perspectives on the future. The timing and ordering of individual future personalized events constitute the "future time perspective" (Doob, 1971; Frank, 1939; Kastenbaum, 1961; Lewin, 1951). The reference is to the number of future personalized events listed in a free response situation and their distribution over various subzones of the future time dimension. A person who anticipates that the most important events in his or her life would be occurring relatively soon is deemed to have a "near" future time perspective. A person with a "distant" future time perspective is one who anticipates that similar events would occur relatively later in life. This classification has been made the basis of a modified version of the Experiential Inventory used extensively by various researchers (e.g., Cottle, 1968, 1976; El Sawy, 1983; Marcus, 1976).

4
PLANNING
HORIZONS

HORIZON SETTING PROCESS

In sharp contrast with the setting of planning objectives, the topic of how planning horizons are determined in business organizations is rarely discussed. This is true both in the research area and in the domain of business practice. One can easily discern evidence of this neglect in the absence of any mention of the setting of planning horizons as a process. Almost all texts on strategic management include at best a casual reference, if that, to the existence of planning periods as part of corporate strategic planning. They indicate the differences between short-term and long-term planning. However, the emphasis is on the virtues of long range and strategic thinking, and on the difficulties and pitfalls of translating that thinking into actual corporate practice.

The general approach to the subject of strategic management can be characterized as being overwhelmingly concerned with the planning objectives component of the strategic planning process. The other element -- planning periods -- is hardly recognized in terms of its significant role in the success of the overall planning process.

We contend that this relative neglect can be ascribed to two critical factors. First, it is not appreciated that planning horizons are an intimate and inseparable part of planning objectives. One cannot have a strategy or a strategic objective, with the intention of attaining it through the strategic planning process, without a fairly definite idea of how long a period of time one has in mind. This time period is, in practice, usually considered as widely understood and agreed upon by the corpus of strategy makers. It is also implicitly, and unwittingly, taken as a given.

There is no conscious realization that the process of setting planning objectives is unavoidably intertwined with the temporal element. This linkage needs to discussed for a complete and balanced understanding of the strategic planning process. The interdependency of planning objectives and planning horizons can be explicated in terms of a goal-means complex. Planning horizons can be visualized as the means component in the goal-means trade-off matrix. We shall elaborate on this subject in Chapter 15, in the hope that practicing executives will become fully aware of the critical temporal element inherent in the process of setting planning objectives.

The second important reason why planning horizons have not been considered as problematic is the lack of adequate attention to the temporal makeup of all decision makers. Perhaps the research establishment has more to blame for this omission than the practicing executives. It is clear from the strategic management literature that the future orientations of strategy makers have not been considered as a factor which enters into the traditional decision making calculus. Obviously, the temporal factor becomes particularly crucial for planning decisions, as the planning process owes its very existence to the future time dimension.

In this chapter, we shall discuss certain critical, but neglected, aspects of planning horizons. The underlying concept is the temporal orientation of strategy makers in the largely unexamined process of setting planning horizons. In the sections that follow, we shall discuss the relevance of the temporal dimension to strategic management, the nature of temporal horizons, the choice of planning horizons, and the role of individual future time perspectives in horizon setting.

The chapter ends with the derivation of the central research hypothesis of the study, linking individual future time perspectives (discussed in Chapter 3) to preferences for short and long planning horizons. Certain further aspects of this topic will be covered in the concluding chapter for ease of exposition.

THE TEMPORAL DIMENSION IN STRATEGY MAKING

Business organizations usually have some sort of a plan, whether explicit or not, reflecting a sense of direction for attaining an intended corporate future. The plan

is basically a guide for an organization to function along
the temporal dimension. The process of strategy making is
dynamic in nature. This dynamism can be appreciated only
against the passage of time. Over a decade ago, the astute
editor of a volume of selected papers on long range business
planning was impelled to make the following prefatory
remarks for his reluctantly composed concluding chapter:

> Although this volume covers a great many aspects
> of long-range planning -- and certainly more than
> its preceding editions did -- it does not probe
> one issue that is so vital it can be called a
> dimension of planning. Since no examination of
> this issue can be found in the literature, the
> Editor volunteers some observations on it himself.
>
> The utterly essential dimension of planning is
> time. ... Yet time is the one dimension of plan-
> ning that never gets discussed. It is treated as
> if it were a constant that everyone understands."
> (Ewing, 1972:439)

Even a cursory reading of the literature on strategy making
would convince us that the temporal dimension continues to
be taken for granted. This is, unfortunately, as true of
managerial practice as of scholarly research.

There is, however, some reason to believe that time is
the primary dimension in the four-dimensional space-time
manifold. In an intriguing paper Navon (1978) makes a
cogent case for a conceptual hierarchy of dimensions, in
which the temporal dimension dominates over the spatial
dimensions. He illustrates this in the following manner:

> The priority of time over space is reflected by
> the fact that language gives time-relations
> greater scope than that of location markers in
> sentences which describe variation over time and
> space; e.g. we might say "The ball was at the
> right corner after it was at the left corner" but
> never "The ball was at t2 to-the-right of where it
> was at t1". In other words, we tend to describe
> motion or displacement as a temporal sequence of
> locations rather than as a spatial string of
> moments. ...
>
> Several observations suggest that our conception
> of the world (or of stimuli in the world) is not a

multidimensional space in which all dimensions
have equal status, but rather a hierarchy of
dimensions, in which time occupies the first level
and spatial dimensions occupy the second one.
(Navon, 1978:226-227)

The notion of the primacy of the time dimension has
also been echoed by other writers, usually along with the
observation that it has been neglected as a serious aspect
of study in the social sciences. Commenting on man's temporality, Kelly (1958:56) has stated:

If man ... exists primarily in the dimensions of
time, and only secondarily in the dimensions of
space, then the terms which we erect for understanding him ought to take primary account of this
view. If we want to know why man does what he
does, then the terms of our whys should extend
themselves in time rather than in space; ...

Apparently, time continues to retain its status as the "hid-
den dimension" of strategy making. In terms of research,
one consequence has been the continuing neglect of the role
of subjective cognition of the future time dimension on the
part of the strategy makers. Ultimately, in order to study
the strategy making process, one has to understand how the
strategy makers, as individuals, fashion that process. To
do so, it is necessary to recognize the role that the individual temporal cognitions play in fashioning the process.

TEMPORAL HORIZONS

As a preliminary to a conceptual understanding of planning periods, it is necessary to consider the essential
nature of temporal horizons. In the words of Taschdjian
(1977:41): "A horizon is a boundary which moves back as we
move toward it. A time horizon is a boundary which sepa-
rates the foreseeable from the unforeseeable future." The
essential nature of a temporal horizon is thus akin to that
of a receding boundary. A somewhat similar notion is evident in Jaques (1982). The description relates to the temporal horizon of an individual in terms of goal-direction:

the temporal horizon of an individual as that goal
among all those toward which he is working at any
given time which has the longest forward targeted

completion time. It is the longest forward planned task in his active present, the farthest forward that he is looking at that moment. The distance of the temporal horizon thus changes as goal-directed episodes are completed and replaced by others, or targeted completion times of existing episodes are changed; just as the distance of the geographical horizon changes with changes in vantage point, or terrain, or visibility. (Jaques, 1982:135).

A conscious intention is evident on the part of the individual to participate in a task lying in the future time zone. It should be noted, though, that this act of intending lies unambiguously in the present time period. The temporal horizon of the individual is determined by the task intended or planned for the most distant period in the future.

We know from the last chapter that the entire future time zone in the mind of the individual is populated by anticipated events. The nature of the temporal horizon is thus dependent on the manner in which the anticipated events and activities are organized. With the progress of time this stream of anticipated events may change in character. However, an individual will always have a temporal horizon associated with the events farthest in anticipation.

One other aspect of temporal horizons in business has to do with the time-span of the environmental feedback that an organization receives. It has been found that this time-span is consistent with that of the temporal orientation of the more effective organizational units (Lawrence and Lorsch, 1967; Lorsch and Morse, 1974). A somewhat different aspect of temporality is revealed by the finding that the maximum time period for which discretion is required to be exercised on a job by an organizational member has a bearing on the felt weight of responsibility (Jaques, 1956, 1961, 1964, 1976).

It would be instructive to consider also the place of temporal horizons in the field of system dynamics (which deals with the behavior of systems through time). According to Perelman (1980), the notion of time is rarely discussed in system dynamics, even though it is clear that there are profound implications arising from the manner in which time is treated and from the time horizon that is selected in the models constructed for policy management. His conclusion about the significance of the temporal dimension in system dynamics, given his perspective of a professional policy analyst, can well be considered as a rationale for the temporal component of the present investigation:

> Our current understanding of time in system dynamics is sharply divided between the pragmatic knowledge of modelers, analysts, and policy makers and the subtle theoretical knowledge of philosophers, mathematicians, physicists, and other scholars who have specialized in the study of time. Both sources must be tapped to improve the treatment of time in system dynamics as it is applied in practice. (Perelman, 1980:88)

It is clear from the foregoing discussion that temporal horizons have an important place in the organizational scheme of things. It is a factor which would need to be accounted for at a level much more explicit than at present.

CHOICE OF PLANNING HORIZONS

The notion of planning periods or planning horizons is clearly related to that of temporal horizons discussed above. However, the precise determination of planning horizons in terms of their appropriate duration is not an easy task. Not only that, the question of appropriateness is itself a problematic issue. This has not been adequately recognized in the literature.

The choice of planning horizons can affect both organizational design and organizational effectiveness (Goodman, 1973). Taylor and Hawkins (1972:61-63) have commented on this point as follows, employing the term "time horizon" to mean what has been specified as "planning horizon" here:

> A significant part of every strategy is the time horizon on which it is based. A viable strategy not only reveals what goals are to be accomplished; it says something about when the aims are to be achieved ...
>
> In choosing an appropriate time horizon, we must pay careful attention to the goals being pursued, and to the particular organisation involved. Goals must be established far enough in advance to allow the organisation to adjust to them. Organisations, like ships, cannot be "spun on a dime." Consequently, the larger the organisation, the further its strategic time horizon must

extend, since its adjustment time is longer. It
is no mere managerial whim that the major contributions to long-range planning have emerged from
the larger organisations ...
      The time horizon is also important because of
its impact on the selection of policies. The
greater the time horizon, the greater the range in
choice of tactics. If, for instance, the goals
desired must be achieved in a relatively short
time, steps like acquisition and merger may become
virtually mandatory.

The early work of Goodman (1967) in the area of
research and development perhaps best serves to bring out
the basic character of the temporal dilemma facing management. Using a multiple case study technique, he examined
the effectiveness of project management versus matrix management forms of organization in the area of manpower utilization in six defense/aerospace contractors in the United
States. His conclusion was that while the project management form of organization was more appropriate than the
matrix management form to handle the numerous short-run
problems normally found in R & D projects, the matrix management form was preferable for the long-run problems. The
following remarks underscore the critical importance of the
time factor in R & D management, but also clearly valid, a
fortiori, to strategy making because of the latter's ineluctable housing within the temporal dimension:

      the dilemma of organizational choice faced by each
      company engaged in research and development prob-
      ably should be dependent primarily upon the prior-
      ities the company places upon the particular
      short-run or long-run time dimensions, and the
      perceived benefits each company anticipates in the
      short run versus the long run. The choice of
      which organizational form to utilize becomes one
      of considerable subjective forecasting and weight-
      ing of anticipated short-run and long-run benefits
      -- obviously a most difficult problem to face.
      (Goodman, 1967:153)

In the field of strategic planning, the "subjective forecasting and weighting" in the above passage probably gains
even more importance. This leads us directly to the notion
that the subjective preference for an appropriate planning
horizon has much to do with the ability of the strategy
maker to "forecast and weigh" things in the future.

The determination of an appropriate planning horizon is dependent on the notion of futurity. The significance of this fact has been emphasized by Drucker (1972:13) in the following words:

> To say "long-range" or "short-range" planning implies that a given time span defines the planning; and this is actually how businesses look at it when they speak of a "five-year plan" or a "ten-year plan." But the essence of planning is to make present decisions with knowledge of their futurity. It is the futurity that determines the time span, and not vice versa.

In general, the type of business would have to be considered for judging whether or not the planning horizon is appropriate. The nature of the strategic decisions involved would also influence the characterization of a planning horizon as short or long.

However, individual judgments or perspectives about the future have not been considered in the conventional methods of selecting planning horizons. Some of the criteria evident in the literature for determining planning horizons are expected interest rate (expectations beyond a certain period being meaningless and hence zero), the nature of different organizational goals, the size and growth rate of an organization, forecasting validity, life cycle of product, payback period, lead time between planning and actualization, and accounting period (Friedman and Segev, 1976:87). These criteria reflect an exclusive preoccupation with quantitative measures. They betray a mechanistic conception of the futurity of present decisions. They also fail to account for the future time perspectives of strategy makers.

The determination of planning horizons is obviously an important activity in the strategy making process. It is critical for efficiently allocating corporate resources and directing organizational efforts. It is also a necessary mechanism for balancing the imperatives of short-run and long-range planning. In the field of management, Goodman (1973:215-216) has described the notion of an organizational time horizon as follows:

> A crude definition of organizational time horizon can be teased out of the question, "How far into the future does an organization look before taking conscious action?" The existential pressure placed upon actions by perceived futures can be

thought of as a basic construct and then time
horizon can be defined as the distance into the
future which leads to significant management
action.

As noted above, a certain knowledge of the nature of
the future dimension is needed to be able to determine the
temporal horizon. A heightened sense of the future is
essential to appreciate the futurity of all present decisions. Some individuals, more than others, have a "tacit
knowledge" about the future, to borrow a term coined by
Michael Polanyi (1967). These individuals can perceive,
farther into the future than others, how deviations in current phenomena will occur. This they can do without actually knowing precisely what will happen in the future.
A notion somewhat akin to this has been proposed by
Schon (1983:50-54) under the rubric "knowing-in-action." He
examines the kinds of knowing involved in "non-logical processes" such as an accountant's swift abstraction of significant facts from a balance sheet (Barnard, 1938:305), in
design (Alexander, 1968), in the qualitative appreciations
of situations (Vickers, 1965), in conforming to rules of
phonology and syntax (as in Noam Chomsky's work on linguis-
tics), in the tacit know-how of everyday social interactions
(Schutz, 1962), and in recognition of movement and gesture
(Birdwhistell, 1970). It seems that these are instances of
"knowing more than we can say" (Schon, 1983:51).
In a somewhat similar manner, a tacit knowledge of the
future exists in individuals in varying degrees. Without
such a special grasp of the future, any choice of a planning
horizon would be no better than routine extrapolations of
the current situation. The fact is, however, not only that
all individuals unavoidably have some perspective about the
future, but also fortunately, this very future perspective
brings to the risk-taking decisions something supplementary
to mundane continuations of the past and the present.
It should be mentioned here that the choice of planning
horizons can be considered as a commitment of virtual meta-
resource (like money) or a means in a goal-means trade-off
matrix. This will be discussed in detail in Chapter 15.
The concept of future time perspective, discussed in
Chapter 3, appears to be potentially relevant to the selection of planning horizons. The subjective temporal attributes of strategy makers seem promising for studying
differences in planning horizon preferences. These preferences are of course indicative of the kind of trade-offs
that strategy makers make in computing the anticipated ben-

efits in the future, weighing and balancing the benefits in the short and long time frames.

Planning periods or horizons are ordinarily set in organizations in accordance with conventions and formal procedures (Steiner, 1969:21-25). For instance, a five-year planning horizon is probably most common among firms having long range planning systems. However, there are indications, as this study also finds, that shorter planning horizons may well be considered more appropriate in a faster-changing future.

We will define the planning horizon as the the period of time over which the plan is drawn up. "The rationale of a given horizon is that the time span should be long enough to permit planning for expected growth and for change in strategy, and yet be short enough to make reasonably detailed plans possible" (Sapp, 1980:35). The observation of Goodman (1973:215) is particularly relevant here: "For most organizations there is a time horizon which consciously calls for positive action, all longer plans receiving only lip service." The significance of selecting appropriate organizational planning horizons would be evident from the following further comments:

> A rich knowledge of the immediate environment leads to short-run effectiveness (tactical brilliance) but it may also lead to long-term ineffectiveness. It does this by shortening the organizational time horizon (strategic myopia). This effect tends to create long-term ineffectiveness when there is a mismatch between the present environment and the future environment. Conversely, lessening the richness with which the immediate environment is known lengthens the actual time horizon. This increases the ability to cope with present/future environmental mismatch but at some risk to the present. (Goodman, 1973:225)

The above observations of course apply to organizations considered as whole entities. The orientation of this study, however, is that strategy making is a process in which a wide variety of individuals participate. The planning horizon of an organization is thus the collective outcome of the decisions of all the strategy makers involved. Such a conglomerate view is well reflected in the published literature, although this has not received sufficient emphasis in the research on strategic decision making in business

(Bourgeois, 1980a; Bower and Doz, 1979; Carter, 1971; Hunt, 1966; Johnson, 1985; Kloeze, Molenkamp, and Roelefs, 1980; Lorange, 1980; van Cauwenbergh and van Robaeys, 1980; Wheelwright and Banks, 1979).

The notion that individual strategy makers collectively constitute the organizational temporal horizon provides us with the necessary rationale for considering individual future time perpectives. The individual orientations or predispositions of the corpus of strategy makers about the future would serve to fashion the corporate temporal orientation. The problematic question, largely ignored in research as well as in practice, is that the strategy makers have differing future orientations. At a minimum, this complicates any attempt to understand the dynamics of corporate temporality.

FUTURE TIME PERSPECTIVE AND PLANNING HORIZONS

In critically examining the individual's interest and emotional involvement in the horizon of his own lifetime, Boniecki (1980) infers that the assumed long-term future time perspectives of contemporary Western man is questionable. His analysis of some 200 Australian adults in a research project "exploring man's concern for his future" leads him to the conclusion that "A time horizon of 20 years hence appears too distant for many people to envoke a meaningful concern leading to a concrete behavioral commitment. A period of 10-15 years seems the most distant practical horizon that the contemporary Western man may see as related to his own life experience" (Boniecki, 1980:174).

Researchers in various fields have found that certain tasks, by virtue of their particular time frame, have called for appropriate time perspectives on the part of the decision maker (Ebert and Piehl, 1973; Epton, 1972; Hammond, 1979; Jaques, 1964; Miller, 1959). As Ebert and Piehl (1973:35) observe:

the optimum decision requires that the time horizon of the decision-maker be suited to the time characteristics of the important factors in the decision. By this reasoning the manager may find time horizon a useful basis for selecting personnel to work on particular projects or decisions. In order to do this effectively, he must be able to judge the time orientations of organizational members, identifying which have long and which have short time horizons.

Of course, what the authors refer to as "time horizon" and "time orientation" are general expressions reflecting the essence of what has been termed as "future time perspective" in this study.

It remains true, though, that it would be most advantageous for a business concern to have appropriate planning expertise for different planning horizons. Ideally, an organization would need to have a full repertoire of planning capabilities for attending to strategic decisions relating to varying temporal horizons. This is clearly called for in order for an organization to be in a position to respond to all kinds of perceived environmental developments.

However, strategy makers cannot realistically be expected to have superior expertise for handling matters relating to all future time sub-zones. The author's own experience as a sometime executive indicates that strategy makers are almost always better suited for either shorter or longer planning horizon tasks, but rarely both. And yet a conscious realization of this phenomenon of differential temporal capabilities of executives does not generally exist in the practical world of business. On the contrary, the conduct of the planning function implicitly assumes the presence of such competence on the part of all executives, and relies on this competence in formulating and implementing corporate strategies.

Given the nature of individual future time perspective, one can surmise the possible impact that strategic actors could have in their choices of, for instance, specific time horizons for different strategic planning areas. This impact is no doubt of a subtle nature, granted the "unobtrusive" character of time. Yet the very fact that individual time perspectives could be a factor in one's approach and orientation to the future (the proper realm of strategic planning), suggests that there are individual predilections which influence, however subtly, the choice of such time-related factors as planning cycles or planning horizons.

In the context of a specific time perspective, this subjective orientation to the future would have a tendency to influence one's general view of how things are going to flow in time. A particular attitude towards the future would thus serve to condition one's general view of the nature of future time and constrain one while making choices about, say, the extent of the planning period. For example, a strategy maker who is distant future oriented would be inclined to prefer a longer planning horizon compared to one who is relatively near future oriented. Hence, the assumption of a consensus on appropriate planning horizons does not appear to be valid.

The above discussion leads us to hypothesize that strategy makers with a near future time perspective are likely to prefer a shorter planning horizon when compared to those with distant future time perspective. Complementarily, the latter would be likely to prefer a longer planning horizon. A diagrammatical representation is given in Figure 4.1. In terms of a general hypothesis, this can be stated as follows:

Hypothesis 1: Strategy makers with near future time perspective will prefer a shorter planning horizon than those with distant future time perspective.

As a final point, it should be mentioned that extensive job experience and superior technical competence in one's functional area does not automatically endow a strategy maker with an adequate capability in long range planning. Strategy makers are legion as ardent advocates of formulating strategies over the long haul. Many indeed would appear to be engaging in long range and strategic thinking in actual practice. Kotter (1982b:161), for example, states that the "excellent" performers among 15 general managers that he studied "develop agendas based on more explicit business strategies that address longer time frames." Such a finding, we suggest, does not provide any evidence of the executives possessing the subjective attribute of being able to visualize, comprehend, and grasp the future time zone any better than other executives.

There is reason for believing that these "excellent" performers may not necessarily have the expertise to address strategies pertinent to all time periods. It is not unlikely that a large proportion of these upper-level executives may not have even a fair degree of distant future orientation. Indeed, the probability of some of the subordinate executives having a superior innate grasp of the distant future cannot be ruled out. This is analogous to such attributes as intelligence and risk taking propensity (MacCrimmon and Wehrung, 1986). The unexamined, tacit assumption that there exists a more distant future time perspective in the upper corporate echelons, by virtue merely of their elevated corporate positions, needs to be investigated. After all, the criteria for promotion and compensation of business executives have not so far included any measure of future-oriented expertise or any real long-range

PREFERRED PLANNING HORIZON

Short   Long

```
T
I   Near          |    FIT    |
M   Future        |           |
E                 |           |
                  |           |
P                 |           |
E                 |           |
R         --------+-----------+--------
S                 |           |
P                 |           |
E                 |           |
C                 |           |
T                 |           |
I   Distant       |           |    .  FIT
V   Future        |           |
E                 |           |
```

Figure 4.1: Future Time Perspective and Planning Horizon

thinking and decision making. Hence, the belief or expectation that there is necessarily a concentration of distant future oriented executives at the highest levels may be more a reflection of a heroic preconception about the top executives than an appreciation of real-world conditions. The practical implications of differential future orientations are obvious in terms of selective executive assignments concerning various aspects of the strategy making process. These implications will be discussed later.

5
PLANNING
MILIEUX

Like any other organizational activity, strategic planning involves the making of choices among available alternatives, in terms of the uncertainty over goals and means. Different strategy makers, however, have different individual perceptions of what precisely are the planning objectives of the organization, and what planning horizons are considered appropriate for attaining those strategic goals. Depending upon the nature of their perceptions, individual strategy makers would proceed to adopt appropriate behavior in terms of the broad subjective framework of strategy making outlined in Chapter 2.

DIMENSIONS OF PLANNING MILIEUX

If we consider the planning horizon as one of the critical means in the goal-means configuration in Figure 2.1, the resultant framework can be depicted as in Figure 5.1.

It will be noticed that the conventional goal-means negotiation and trade-off is now in terms of planning objectives and planning horizons. In the last chapter, the justification for treating the organizational planning horizon as a significant means was briefly indicated (with a fuller discussion deferred to Chapter 15). It may also be mentioned that, on the basis of a study of the views of top management teams on corporate objectives and the means to attain them in 12 non-diversified public corporations, Bourgeois (1980a:244) concluded that the "lack of consensus on means is more troublesome than disagreement on ends."

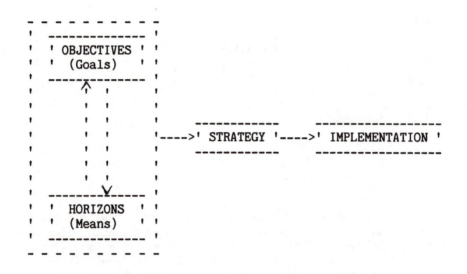

STAGE 1
Perception of
Strategy
Environment

STAGE 3
Strategy
Delineation

STAGE 4
Strategy
Implementation

STAGE 2
Evaluation of
Strategy
Environment

Figure 5.1: Perceptual-Temporal View of Strategy Making

The perceptual connotations of the trade-off process involving planning objectives and planning horizons, as indicated in the leftmost box in Figure 5.1, can best be explicated in terms of a contingency framework. The framework is based on the two major dimensions of perceived degree of agreement about planning objectives and planning horizons among strategy makers.

The first dimension, concerning planning objectives, relates to the degree of agreement among the strategy makers in the organization as perceived by each individual. The second dimension pertains, in a similar fashion, to the degree of agreement about the time period that has been organizationally determined for accomplishing those planned objectives, or the planning horizon.

The resultant matrix formed by dichotomizing the two dimensions, as depicted in Figure 5.2, consists of four quadrants. Each quadrant is an ideal-type internal organizational context of planning as perceived by individual strategy makers. The term suggested for this planning context is "perceived planning milieu." Such a framework should enable us to establish the contingent relationships between the two factors, namely, planning objectives and planning horizons. In brief, the four planning milieux are derived from the different combinations of the perceived level of agreement among strategy makers in general regarding planning objectives and planning horizons.

FUTURE TIME PERSPECTIVE AND PLANNING MILIEUX

It is clear that, irrespective of the degree of perceived agreement about planning objectives, all strategy makers can be separated into two groups, depending on high or low level of perceived agreements on planning horizon. The first group, in reference to the matrix in Figure 5.2, consists of those strategy makers who by definition would perceive Planning Milieux I and II, while the second Planning Milieux III and IV.

Recalling the discussion on individual future time perspective (Chapter 3), it is clear that those who have a "distant" future time perspective would be more likely to perceive more disagreement, or less agreement, about planning horizons compared to those whose perspective is only "near." This is so because, having a relatively "near" perspective, the strategy makers concerned would perceptually "condense" and "telescope" the entire gamut of potential alternatives and choices of feasible planning horizons onto

PLANNING OBJECTIVES

	High Agreement	Low Agreement
PLANNING HORIZONS High Agree-ment	I	II
Low Agree-ment	III	IV

Figure 5.2: Types of Planning Milieux

a relatively small event-canvass. Citing the work of Epton (1972) in the area of research and development projects, Twiss (1980:129) has observed: "Task completion dates are unconsciously predicted within the time horizon of the estimator, leading to underestimation of the duration of projects extending beyond this time horizon."

The "limited temporality" or "limited futurity" that is indicated above means that there is a relatively small arena of potential differences of temporal choices among strategy makers. This would constrain a "near" FTP strategy maker into perceiving less in the way of room for disagreement. Which, of course, translates to high perceived agreement in the terminology employed here. Thus the "near" FTP strategy makers would be more likely to perceive Planning Milieux I and II. The converse applies to the "distant" FTP strategy makers. In terms of a general hypothesis, this may be stated as follows:

Hypothesis 2: Strategy makers with a near future time perspective will perceive Planning Milieux I and II more than III and IV, while those with a distant future time perspective will perceive Planning Milieux III and IV more than I and II.

Employing an identical reasoning for strategic actors separated into two groups based on high and low level, respectively, of perceived agreement on planning objectives, it would follow that the "near" FTP strategy makers would be more likely to perceive Planning Milieux I and III, and complementarily for the "distant" FTP strategy makers. This leads to the following:

Hypothesis 3: Strategy makers with a near future time perspective will perceive Planning Milieux I and III more than II and IV, while those with a distant future time perspective will perceive Planning Milieux II and IV more than I and III.

The preceding two hypotheses, if confirmed, would help us link the construct of future orientation of individuals with their perception of the nature of internal planning context. The potential implications of this, to be explored later, are clearly related to the overall managerial concern about how individual executives tend to interpret the same planning situation in different ways.

DIFFERENCES IN PERCEIVED CONSENSUS ON PLANNING OBJECTIVES AND PLANNING HORIZONS

In keeping with the general thrust of the discussion above, it would also be reasonable to hypothesize that the overall level of agreement perceived by strategy makers regarding planning horizons would be lower than that regarding planning objectives. This is only to be expected because the notion of planning horizon is, as has been argued here, traditionally given considerably less importance on a conscious level by strategic actors, and is not one for which there is general and widespread awareness. This very ambiguity -- engendered and sustained by organizational inattention and cultivated ignorance -- would be most likely to lead to a general perception of lack of agreement among organizational members.

The case of planning objectives would be somewhat different on account of more extensive awareness of their nature and content in the organizational context. This is not in any way to state that there would be a high level of agreement on planning objectives per se, but only to contend that greater familiarity of the notion of planning objectives would result in a general perception of a higher level of prevailing consensus. It is the perceptions of strategy makers that concerns us here, and these perceptions of consensus or otherwise would, it is argued, differ as between planning objectives and planning horizons. This can be stated in the following terms:

> Hypothesis 4: Strategy makers will perceive less agreement prevailing among organizational members concerning planning horizons than concerning planning objectives.

One of the implications of this hypothesis, if proven, is that organizational members may feel less motivated to exert effort in a perceived environment substantial disagreement and confusion. Executives would not feel total commitment to objectives which they perceive are not shared. Likewise, they would not be totally convinced that particular objectives are to be achieved within certain time frames if there is a perception of comparative dissensus about planning horizons among the personnel involved. The implication clearly is that managements need to recognize this built-in perceptual constraint among organizational members and institute suitable steps to achieve a greater degree of perceived consensus. Further comments on this subject will be made after examining the data in Chapters 10 and 15.

PLANNING MILIEUX AND DECISION MODES

Looking at another aspect of perceived planning milieux, it appears from the literature that each milieu would tend to invite a specific type of decision mode in the planning process. For instance, by considering the two dimensions of "preferences about possible outcomes" and "beliefs about causation," and dichotomizing them for certainty and uncertainty, a four-fold typology has been constructed (Thompson, 1964, 1967; Thompson and Tuden, 1959). The authors have suggested that a specific decision strategy (among what they termed as computation, compromise, judgment, and inspiration) would be appropriate for each of the four cells in the matrix. Nalbandian and Klingner (1980) have examined the utility of this framework (in a slightly modified form) in the area of public personnel administration and found that the different decision contexts did indeed help in understanding the associated decision strategies.

In the present investigation, the planning milieu typology has been constructed in a slightly different form from those of Thompson and others. First, the two dimensions are of the traditional goal-means type, and second, the dimensions are dichotomized in terms of high and low perceived agreement. This seems more relevant to the question of how strategy makers perceived the internal organizational context, in preference to the dichotomy of certainty-uncertainty (Thompson, 1964, 1967) or of agree-disagree (Nalbandian and Klingner, 1980).

As applied to strategic planning, therefore, one would expect to find Planning Milieu I as the one likely to be perceived by those strategy makers who believe that the planning objectives are known and agreed upon by most strategy makers in the organization, and that the planning horizons for accomplishing those objectives are also known and widely agreed upon. In relation to electronic banking, the particular forum for this study, this type may include such planning areas as funds management policies. The existence of set policies and procedures for electronic funds transfer operations may well generate an impression of consistency. While commercial banks are always striving to improve upon their efficiency in terms, say, of the volume of float, the strategic thinking usually is relatively straightforward, consisting of refining internal procedures, aiming for productivity gains over specific periods, investing in telecommunications equipment, and the like. Hence the planning milieu would most likely be perceived as one where the

appropriate mode of decision making is one of "standardization," namely, a method which is routine and where standard
procedures exist and are applicable most often.

Where the planning objectives are perceived as uncertain or subject to disagreement, yet the planning horizons
for the accomplishment of the different objectives seem
agreed upon, which is Planning Milieu II, one would expect
the planning milieu to be inviting the appropriate decision
making mode of "negotiation," which is characterized by
give-and-take and bargaining. That could happen, for
instance, in the area of a management information systems
framework being planned for a bank. While the top management may agree upon the organization's need to develop and
implement a sophisticated management information system
within a short period of time, say, 3 years, it is not
unlikely that the precise objectives of the project would
engender considerable differences of opinion. This could be
in the area of the level of sophistication in the furnishing
of processed information to executives, the amount of
resources justifiable (assuming enough is available within
reason), and so on. The incidence of organizational politics, while ubiquitous, is likely to be more overt in this
type of planning milieu than in others.

In Planning Milieu III, while the planning objectives
seem to be agreed upon, there is some disagreement perceived
about the planning horizon to achieve those objectives. The
installation schedule for automated teller machines (ATMs)
may belong to this category. The perception of how the competition is doing, the urge to keep up with the Joneses, the
readiness to incur the premium expenditure involved in
accelerated installation of the machines, etc. are some factors that are weighed largely according to individual preferences. Here too, as in Planning Milieu II, the
appropriate mode for making the planning decisions would be
that of "negotiation." Unlike in Planning Milieu II,
though, the negotiation in Planning Milieu III is over the
speed with which the planning objectives should be implemented and attained.

It needs to be emphasized at this point that, having
regard to the intrinsic nature of the strategic planning
function, negotiation as a decision mode should be quite
prevalent in all the four planning milieux. This is so
because the process of strategic planning is seen as substantively informed with give-and-take, compromise, and bargaining. These negotiating activities would be likely to be
perceived as endemic to the strategic planning exercise, and
so one would not expect the decision mode of negotiation to

be overly dominant in any particular planning milieu. The differentiation of the other two decision modes, though, is expected to be distinct as between Planning Milieux I and IV, and a discussion of the latter milieu follows.

In Planning Milieu IV, there is a lack of consensus in both the planning objectives and planning horizons, and usu-ally comprise fuzzy or "squishy" problems (Strauch, 1975). This could be the case, for example, in regard to the devel-opment of new services for consumers. The entire question of the scope and extent of electronification of consumer services, the degree of sophistication in technology, the budgetary allocation that could be justified in relation to the demands of other corporate activities, the estimate of present and future competition, are all critical matters needing careful consideration. And yet, precisely because of the ambiguous nature of the data available for this kind of decisions, as well as differing subjective preferences for desirable organizational plans in any of such areas, the strategy makers would be likely to adopt a mixed mode of decision strategies, which has been termed here as "subjec-tive," for want of a more fitting descriptive term. The basic point in this type of planning milieu is that there is no particular decision strategy that is dominant or uniquely appropriate, other than the fact that the decision making mode is dictated largely by subjective values and prefer-ences, in which people use analogic reasoning and often have to follow hunches, intuitions, and opinions (e.g., see Agor, 1984; Barnard, 1938; Bateson, 1972; Isaack, 1978; Isenberg, 1984; March, 1976; Mintzberg, 1976; Pondy, 1984; Rowan, 1986; Wagner, 1978; Watzlawick, Weakland, and Fisch, 1974; Weick, 1977).

The proposed framework, represented diagrammatically in Figure 5.3, should enhance the understanding of actual modes of decision making that strategy makers perceive as being used in the strategic planning process, and evaluate their appropriateness. It is clear that given certain perceptions of the planning milieu by individual strategy makers, spe-cific decision modes are selected in practice. The frame-work should thus allow us to gain insight into whether strategic actors are indeed selecting the appropriate deci-sion strategies or whether inappropriate ones are being adopted.

Flowing from the above discussion, and in keeping with the subjective approach to the strategic planning process, it needs to be examined whether different decision modes are likely to be perceived as more prevalent in different plan-ning milieux. The following hypotheses are proposed to assist the analysis:

PLANNING OBJECTIVES

		High Agreement	Low Agreement
P L A N N I N G H O R I Z O N S	High Agree- ment	I Standardization	II Negotiation
	Low Agree- ment	III Negotiation	IV Subjective

Figure 5.3: Planning Milieux and Decision Modes

Hypothesis 5: Strategy makers in Planning Milieu I will perceive the use of "standardization" decision mode more than the strategy makers in Planning Milieu IV.

Hypothesis 6: Strategy makers in Planning Milieu IV will perceive the use of "subjective" decision mode more than the strategy makers in Planning Milieu I.

The implications of the preceding two hypotheses for strategic management are primarily in the area of how executives select their own decision making mode. The fact that an executive perceives a particular decision mode predominant in the organization is very likely to influence that selection. This insight about the adoption of individual decision modes on the basis of perceptions of the overall decision modes prevailing in the planning process should prove helpful to top managements for instituting changes where necessary. In sum, the presumption that uniform decision modes prevail in the strategy making process may not be warranted. More to the point, these modes may be selected by individual executives on the basis of what they perceive about the nature of the planning milieux.

PART III
RESEARCH METHODOLOGY AND RESULTS

6
RESEARCH
METHODOLOGY

THE SETTING

The study was conducted in the commercal banking industry. A homogeneous population was necessary as the emphasis of the inquiry was on the dynamics of individual perceptions of different organizational members. A single industry was therefore appropriate. The banking industry was selected for the additional reason that the author had extensive experience as an executive in one of the world's largest international commercial banking organizations. This experience proved advantageous in establishing a high level of rapport with top executives helping to facilitate the study or participating in it. Familiarity with the peculiar language and terminology of the banking industry, and a sense of its distinctive culture, was of decided benefit in conducting the investigation.

Two of the largest ("top 10") commercial banks in the U.S. were selected as research sites, although only one bank would have sufficed for the primary objectives of the investigation. The second sample, somewhat smaller compared to the first, was added to see whether the findings from the first body of research data were sustainable with the replication. The primary, larger sample is from a bank (named here as WESTBANK) which operated predominantly in the western part of the United States, while the second, smaller sample was from a bank operating mainly in the eastern part of the country (named here as EASTBANK). The constitution and nature of the two samples are detailed later. Large banks were selected so that an adequate number of executives would be available to furnish the requisite subjective and other data relating to the same kind of organizational arena.

Besides the two banks which finally served as research sites, two other banks were also initially explored for the same purpose. One of these banks thought that the number of executives desired in the sample for the questionnaire survey was much beyond what they could reasonably spare for the purpose, and hence could not agree to participate. The other bank seemed to the author to lack the necessary commitment for the satisfactory completion of the research project.

Top management support and wide participation by the top executives were considered essential by this researcher, and hence the selectivity in bank sites. The alternative would have been, not for the last time, one more investigation of a patently top level corporate phenomenon being studied through the unrealistic responses of university students and the like. Plainly, students and other subjects with no high-level corporate experience would be most unlikely to be able to adopt a strategy maker role with any verisimilitude. For it is through a succession of demanding role episodes (Katz and Kahn, 1978) that an organizational member can acquire the peculiar attitudes, values, thought patterns, and behaviors that go with a position or role.

While it is true that two of the four banks were not selected for the study -- and only one suitable research site was all that was needed for the investigation --, it should be noted that the executives of all the four banks approached at different times served quite willingly and competently as consultants in reviewing the questionnaire and suggesting valuable amendments.

Strategic planning in the area of electronic banking was selected for investigation. The reason for this choice was that a single, clearly delineated and widely understood area of actviity constituted the notion of planning content more appropriately than an entire strategic plan. The area of electronic banking denoted a commonly-shared planning universe. It was also necessary for all strategy makers to be able to concentrate on a specific area for eliciting the desired information. A full-fledged strategic plan, in all its comprehensiveness, would be too diverse an attention area to generate a shared arena for investigating subjective appreciations of the strategy makers.

BACKGROUND NOTES ON ELECTRONIC BANKING

It would facilitate the appreciation of this investigation if a few brief points are made at this stage about the historical background of electronic banking and its impact on the commercial banking industry.

Commercial banks in the U.S., as elsewhere, have traditionally been restricted through governmental regulations in regard to the kinds of financial services they are permitted to offer. For instance, regulations prohibited these banks from engaging in the underwriting of securities and certain insurance services.

Against the historical background of regulations, commercial banks (such as the ones involved in this study) were constrained to differentiate their depository, payments, and lending services on the basis of "convenience" to their customers. This has been the story in most countries over the past few decades. Commercial or full service banks are, by the very nature of their service, organizations in which the physical presence of customers has a dominant influence on the efficiency of the system. Deprived of the usual pricing option on account of Regulation Q (which fixed ceilings on permissible interest rates that banks could quote), competition for providing this convenience mostly took the form of easy customer access to banking services. This naturally meant the establishment of an extensive branch network to service the potential clientele in as many localities as possible. Geographical propinquity to customers became the most potent way of competing and procuring new business.

The banks were obliged to continue with this strategy, having no better alternative, despite the fact that it inevitably created problems of administrative control. The desideratum of an extensive branch network implied the maintenance of a large contingent of personnel to provide both personal service and full service facilities to all customers. The traditional product differentiation strategy thus consisted of the twin dove-tailed components of geographical proximity to customers and provision of personal and full service banking.

This apparently high-cost approach to delivering banking services was possible because of the availability of relatively cheap customer deposits (flowing from Regulation Q cited earlier). The assured supply of low-cost deposits -- the raw material of banking -- enabled banks to enjoy a large spread vis-a-vis the (unregulated) interest rates on loans they were free to charge, subject only to usury laws. The regulations, in effect, ensured both cartel-like conditions and relatively unworrisome profit making avenues. The usury laws of various states, it seems, constitute an important aspect of the regulatory environment which affects the branching policies of banks in terms of locational quasi-rents.

This somewhat placid situation has been changing radically in the last few years through developments in two significant areas. The first one is that of general deregulation of banking, but especially of interest rates. The second area, central to this note, has to do with the technological advances in electronic funds transfer systems (EFTS).

The progressive deregulation of banks started with the passage of the Depository Institutions Deregulation and Monetary Control Act of 1980. (For a recent assessment of the bank regulatory policy, see Kareken (1986)). Under deregulation, bank managements have to determine the deposit interest rate in order to maximize their profitability through greater interest margin, trading off higher interest rates on deposits (for attracting a higher volume) against more interest revenue from employing the additional deposits in earning assets. The key seems to be competitive pricing. The pricing game, however, involves many factors, not the least of which is the exposure to the volatility of the competitive interest rates in the financial marketplace. Overall, the trend is towards greater competition, less profitability, and more failures and forced mergers. Other kinds of financial service intermediaries, such as investment banks, insurance firms, savings and loans, thrifts, etc., are growing in strength, and are expected to offer increasing competition to commercial banks in the future (Balderston, 1985; Fraser and Kolari, 1985; Sontheimer and Thorn, 1986).

The essence of EFTS is that many kinds of banking transactions could be satisfactorily carried out without the constraints of either geographical proximity or specified business hours. Naturally, the traditional calculus of customer convenience (branch network, operating hours, personal service) is being rapidly replaced by the EFTS and telephone-based delivery systems. Greater thought is being given to the rationalization of branch banking. It is quite on the cards that banks may indeed close down some of their existing branches, saving on operating costs and relying more on higher interest rates to compete.

One of the difficulties of the rapid expansion of electronic technology, and the proliferation of new products and services that flows from that, has been the increased risk of fraud and employee errors. Banks are thus required to insure themselves against such risks and financial loss, and take steps to avoid or minimize the chances of fraud by better training of personnel, physical security, encryption, authentication protocol, reporting procedures, audit trails, etc. Technological advances are also increasingly prompting the financial institutions to assume greater risks than in the past, although the regulatory agencies now have more efficient means to supervise and control (Saunders and White, 1986).

The indications are that advances in the area of technology for banking services would be sustained in the foreseeable future. The "smart card," for instance, is expected to replace the existing credit cards and personal checks in the next decade. This microprocessor card, invented in France, is being extensively experimented in that country for point-of-sale transactions at many banks and other financial institutions, for telepayments in a videotex environment (for home banking, mail ordering, seat reservations, etc.), and public telephone payment. Similar trials are in progress in other European countries. In the U.S., plans for experimentation of the smart card are in the process of being finalized. The adoption of the smart card in the next few years seems almost certain, and the commercial banks have hardly any choice but to convert to electronic banking in a fairly total sense.

Another development that is expected in retail electronic banking is that of increased sharing of networks to expand geographic reach, based principally on the current ATMs but also later around home-bound delivery systems.

It is clear that banks have of necessity to concentrate on achieving continuous improvements in communications and information management if they are to stay competitive. Considerable efforts have traditionally been made to apply operations research and management science techniques in banking for improving efficiency. A new information environment is being generated through technological changes, and banks have perforce to keep pace with them. At present, though, there appears to be a considerable technological confusion among all management levels, affecting profitability.

The deregulation phase has been coupled with increasing turbulence in the external environment of banks, both domestically and in the international sphere. It is generally agreed that banks need to go in for strategic planning in a comprehensive manner, and one notes the frequent discussions of the subject in the banking literature.

RESEARCH SAMPLE

The data were collected from a large section of the executives working at different levels in the headquarters of the two selected commercial banks. The widest possible coverage of strategy makers within the same bank was considered essential to ensure that sufficient data were generated for meaningful comparisons between the two major categories of future time perspective. Data gathering was primarily through a questionnaire developed specially for the survey (see Appendix A). This is discussed in the next section. The survey data were supplemented by background knowledge obtained through personal interviews, archival records, and industry literature.

The target population was top executives of the two banks, consisting of only those who had corporate titles of Executive Vice President, Senior Vice President, Vice President, and Assistant Vice President. However, while in the case of the WESTBANK, the primary sample for this research, executives throughout the corporate headquarters were made available for the project, the EASTBANK authorities allowed only two units of their corporate headquarters for the purpose. While these two units were very large in their personnel component, the restricted nature of the second sample allowed only Vice Presidents and Assistant Vice Presidents to be sampled, there being an insufficient number of members in the two higher organizational levels.

For WESTBANK, a stratified random sample was selected so as to abide by the limit of 300 executives agreed upon with the authorities. This number was considered quite adequate for purposes of testing the research hypotheses. The directory of managerial level employees of the bank (printed for internal office use only), which contained the corporate as well as functional titles of all executives at corporate headquarters, was utilized for selecting randomly the requisite numbers of executives at each organizational level. A reminder was also sent to the defaulting subjects after about a month. The specific numbers of questionnaires sent out and responses received are detailed in a subsequent section.

In the case of EASTBANK, the major portion of negotiations relating to the research project were carried out with officials at the bank's regional office in a western city. The subjects, though, worked at the corporate headquarters located in the eastern part of the country. All the executives in the two corporate units were available as research subjects, and all were sent questionnaires. However, no reminders were sent to the defaulting subjects.

One of the principal aims of this investigation was to obtain data from executives at the highest levels of an organization. The sample finally obtained realized this objective fully, and involved several months of prelimiinary discussions with officials of four of the country's top international commercial banking organizations. A second, concurrent aim was to have the questionnaires sent under cover of an internal official communication from a senior executive, and this too was achieved.

SURVEY QUESTIONNAIRE DEVELOPMENT

The questionnaire administered to the bank executives was sent under cover of a letter. The items in the survey questionnaire relevant to the research reported in this book are contained in Appendix A.

One important aspect of the questionnaire had to do with the clear delineation of the subject-matter of electronic banking. Arising out of the discussions with various bank executives, it seemed that the most effective way of eliciting reasoned responses about electronic banking was to select a few of its substantive sub-areas. Such an approach would obviate the possible haziness in the minds of subjects about what precisely constitutes electronic banking. The next step was to identify the most pertinent sub-areas for strategic planning in electronic banking. These sub-areas are referred to simply as "areas" or "aspects" in the questionnaire for the benefit of the respondents.

Extensive discussions about this matter were carried out by the author with senior bank executives, and the following five sub-areas were identified as the most appropriate: Electronic Funds Tranfer, Electronic Cash Management, Automated Data Processing Capacity, Electronic Mail, and Telecommunications. The consensus among the bank executives consulted was that there were a few other aspects of electronic banking which could be and are considered for strategic planning purposes, such as Automated Teller Machines, On-line Information Systems, Accounting Information Delivery Systems, Regional Data Processing and Entry, Product Planning, and Operations Development. However, the five sub-areas selected constituted the core at the present time in terms of strategic planning for electronic banking. Furthermore, it was felt that these sub-areas were widely understood, although not uniformly widespread in practice, by the executives at large and would thus pose no problems in shared comprehension.

All items in the questionnaire were finalized after consultations on the lines described above. Most importantly, great care was taken to ensure that the wordings of the questions were easily understood by the bank executives.

It should be added here that the question on future time perspective (Question 13) evoked some reservations on the part of the executives on the ground that its content seemed irrelevant to strategic planning. This reaction was understandable; but since the author was not free to disclose the significance of the data in terms of the hypothesized relationships with other "traditionally accepted planning factors," all that could be done was to persuade the bank officials concerned to permit inclusion of the question (appropriately worded for clear comprehension), and hope that not too many respondents are "turned off" by it. As subsequent experience showed, some of the executives did indeed omit answering this question, on the basis of irrelevance rather than incomprehension. However, for the purpose of ensuring a good overall response rate among busy top executives, the author had deemed it critical to negotiate with the appropriate bank officials for the questionnaire to be served under cover of an internal office memorandum. The memorandum stated, inter alia, that the research project had the approval of one of the Executive Vice Presidents of the bank. Having been a sometime bank executive, the author believed that this was the most effective way of inviting the participation of an organization's senior executives. The encouraging response rate could be attributed at least in part to this approach.

OPERATIONALIZATIONS OF VARIABLES

The contents of the questionnnaire and the operationalizations of the variables employed in this study are discussed below. As a matter of convenience, the variables are discussed in conjunction with the questionnaire items in the order they appear in the survey questionnaire (see Appendix A), along with other derived variables at the appropriate places. A complete list of the variables, together with the respective acronyms in block capitals, is given in Table 6.1.

Question 1 related to the corporate title of the respondent, to determine the organizational level (ORGLEVEL) at which the executive works. The four extant titles were combined to constitute three organizational levels. Values of 1, 2, and 3 were assigned, respectively, to the corporate

TABLE 6.1

List of Variables in the Study

Variable Description	Variable Acronym	Questionnaire Location
1. Sex	SEX	Q 17
2. Age	AGE	Q 18
3. Education level	EDUCATL	Q 19
4. Functional area	FUNCAREA	Q 3
5. Organizational level	ORGLEVEL	Q 1
6. Job experience	JOBEXP	Q 6
7. Preferred planning horizon	PLGHOR	Q 10
8. Future time perspective	FTP	Q 13
9. Agreement perceived on planning objectives of bank	AGROBJ	Q 14
10. Agreement perceived on planning horizon of bank	AGRHOR	Q 15
11. Mode of decision making in bank is perceived as "standardization"	STANDARD	Q 16
12. Mode of decision making in bank is perceived as "negotiation"	NEGOTN	Q 16
13. Mode of decision making in bank is perceived as "subjective"	SUBJECT	Q 16

titles of Assistant Vice President (AVP), Vice President (VP), and a joint category of Executive Vice President and Senior Vice President (ESVP). The latter joint group was constituted for purposes of this study in order to have a sizable number of subjects in the sample, as the total number of Executive Vice Presidents in WESTBANK was relatively small. This smallness in the number of Executive Vice Presidents would have tended to render possible, after a fashion, informed conjectures about the identity of the respondents and the nature of their responses, thus engendering a sense of abridgment of the complete confidentiality requirement. It should be noted, though, that the EASTBANK replication sample did not have the ESVP category (see Chapter 13).

Question 2 elicited the functional title of the subject. This was included in the questionnaire only as an additional check on the identity of the respondent for purposes of follow-up, but perhaps more importantly, as a way to segue unambiguously into the next question about functional area. The information generated from this particular item was thus not utilized for any analysis. For readers not au courant with the wide variety of activities in a large commercial bank, the prolixity of functional titles could well appear bewildering. It may be of some value to glance over a selection of the functional titles of respondents in this study, to facilitate a degree of comprehension of the intricate web of operational and administrative activities at a bank's corporate headquarters. The following sampling is offered to that end, listed in no particular order:

    Advanced Systems & Technology Manager
    Senior Research Analyst
    General Accounting & Regulatory Reporting Section Head
    Applications Consultant
    Product Manager
    Technical Procedures Officer
    Money Market Unit Supervisor
    Senior Credit Review Officer
    Instruction & Development Manager
    Deputy Territory Administrator
    Senior Accounting Policy Analyst
    Strategic Planning & Administrative Division Manager
    Government Guaranteed Loan Division Manager
    Senior Information Systems Officer
    Corporate Reporting & Accounting Section Manager
    Consumer Loans Administrator
    Automated Data Processing Group Administrator

Senior Program Designer
Operations Coordinator
Corporate Banking Account Officer
Database Management Section Manager
Domestic Money Services Section Manager
Credit Review Department Head
Confirmation Section Supervisor
Planning & Marketing Officer
Branch Banking Division Administrator
Electronic Banking Unit Manager
Correspondent Bank Officer
Global Operations Project Manager
Acquisition & Sales Division Manager
International Operations Analyst
Interbank Adjustments Officer
Management Communications Division Manager
International Automated Services Section Manager
Senior Commercial Loan Documentation Control Officer
Cash Mobilization Section Supervisor
Domestic Communications Services Manager

Question 3 was concerned with the functional area of responsibility (FUNCAREA) of the subject. This was the only question in which a different set of categories had to be used for the two research samples. In the case of WESTBANK, the main site, the directory of executives from which the subjects were selected permitted the classification of all positions into the nine functional groupings officially employed by the bank and a tenth ("other") group created by merging together the sundry remaining functional units. These ten categories were: Branch Banking (item nomenclature masked), International Banking, Corporate Banking, Financial Management, Credit, Staff Support, Management Services, Automated Data Processing, Planning & Marketing, and Others (including Audit, Legal, etc.). Respondents were presented with the list of ten functional categories and were asked to circle the one to which they belonged. The functions performed under each of these ten categories are broadly reflected in their names. Taken as a package, the ten categories should facilitate an appreciation of the flavor of commercial banking -- the activity in which the subject executives were engaged.

For the EASTBANK sample, the subjects belonged primarily to the functional area of international banking. However, instead of omiting this question altogether, it was decided to elicit a different kind of information, namely, in terms of administrative, credit, marketing, operations, personnel, product development, and the remainder category of "other."

Question 6 asked for the number of years of job experience (JOBEXP) that the subject has had in the organization.

Question 10 was concerned with the key variable relating to the preferred planning horizon (PLGHOR). The object was to ascertain what length of time (in years) that each individual executive considers as most appropriate for drawing up plans for the bank in the area of electronic banking. As this question involved a critical variable in the study, considerable attention was paid to making certain that the respondents would have no difficulty in clearly understanding what information was being solicited. As indicated in the section on questionnaire development, extensive discussions with knowledgable top executives of four banks and subsequent pilot testing for easy comprehension of the question's import were carried out before arriving at the following wording for the initial part of the item:

> What do you believe is the most appropriate time period for which plans should be drawn up in your bank (in terms of performance goals, resource allocation, organizational actions, etc.) in each of the following areas of electronic banking?

Also on the basis of the discussions mentioned above, it was decided to add the following explanatory note in parentheses about the nature of the planning period to facilitate better grasp of what was being sought:

> (This time period should be long enough to permit planning for expected growth and for changes in strategy, and yet be short enough to make reasonably detailed plans possible.)

This parenthetical addendum was adapted from Sapp (1980), and was received well by the bank executives who were consulted. It may be noticed that the term "planning horizon" has not been used in the questionnaire. This was done so as not to introduce any apparently technical term that was not common coinage in the distinctive argot of commercial banking.

A further part of the question provided the subject with a choice of stating the preferred planning period either as a straightforward number of years, such as "3", or as a range of years, such as "2 to 3" or "9 to 11". This was done to facilitate the response, so that both a specific

number and a range estimate would be equally acceptable. It
turned out, though, that very few subjects opted for a range
of years in their response. Thus the exploratory analysis,
intended originally, of whether there was a potential difference between the subjects who chose a specific number of
years vis-a-vis those who selected a range could not be carried out. The planning horizon was computed as the mean of
the range extremes where this option was exercised by the
few subjects. Furthermore, the preferred planning horizon
(PLGHOR) of each subject was calculated by taking the average of the data furnished for the five sub-areas of electronic banking (discussed earlier in the section on
questionnaire development).

Question 13 dealt with another key variable of the
study, namely, the future time perspective (FTP). The question was adapted from Cottle (1968). The adaptation consisted mainly in the substitution of the "future" time
period for the all-inclusive "past, present, and future"
span used by Cottle. A minor change consisted in not
insisting that the subjects write down the description of
the future event in the questionnaire. This information was
of no importance or use for the present study. More to the
point, it was found that the bank executives consulted while
finalizing and testing the questionnaire were of the opinion
that executives at large would be somewhat hesitant and
uncomfortable about writing down the descriptions of the
significant future events in their lives, such as expected
promotion, divorce, career change, death, etc.
Incidentally, in a few cases, the respondents nevertheless
wrote down the future events on the questionnaires.

The question asked the bank executives to make a list
of nine important events that they expected would happen in
the future in their own personal lives. Cottle had provided
for ten experiences. In the discussions with bank officials
responsible for permitting the research to be carried out,
it transpired that nine events would be more acceptable as
it gave the impression of a tolerably small single-digit
number -- a factor considered to be of some weight in terms
of lesser perceived effort on the part of the busy senior
executives. Cottle and Klineberg (1974:107) have observed
that the figure of ten experiences is an arbitrary one, but
that what matters about developing this kind of an inventory
is that the number of items should be sufficient for the
intended purpose without being too much of a burden for the
respondent.

To facilitate the listing of the nine events, it was
suggested to the subjects that they may jot down one or two

identifying words on a separate sheet of paper as an aide memoire. After this listing was done, they were asked to categorize each of those events into one of the following four time periods which best represents the occurrence of the event: (1) very near future (FTPVNEAR), (2) near future (FTPNEAR), (3) distant future (FTPDIST), and (4) very distant future (FTPVDIST). Columns headed with these descriptive time periods were provided so that the subjects could easily circle the appropriate column number against each event. The specific wording of the question ran as follows:

Now a somewhat different kind of topic. On a separate sheet of paper, please list nine important events you expect to happen in your own personal life in the future. You only need to jot down one or two words for each such expected event for your ease of identification.

After you have listed all nine events, select the time period that best represents the occurrence of each event. Indicate this by circling the appropriate column number.

The FTP score of each subject was calculated by taking the average of the values furnished for the nine events. A value of 1 is assigned to an event in the "very near" future subzone, a value of 2 to an event in the "near" subzone, and so on. The FTP score could thus range from a possible minimum of 1 (when all the nine events are placed in the "very near" subzone) to a maximum of 4 (when all the nine events are deposited in the "very distant" subzone).

Question 14 sought to elicit the perception of the respondent about the extent to which the managerial staff in the organization were in agreement about the planned objectives (AGROBJ) of electronic banking in each of the five sub-areas. The degree of this perceived consensus was captured by a 5-point Likert-type scale, as follows: (1) no agreement at all, (2) very little agreement, (3) moderate agreement, (4) substantial agreement, and (5) complete agreement. The wording of the question was as follows:

I would like you to think about how different people view the objectives of electronic banking. To what extent do you believe the managerial staff in your bank are in agreement about the planned objectives of electronic banking in each area?

The average of the five values indicated by the subject was calculated to provide the response for this question.

Question 15 was on the same lines as the earlier one, and dealt specifically with perceived agreement about the planning periods or planning horizons (AGRHOR), using the same 5-point scale. Again, the average of the values indicated by the subject for the five sub-areas of electronic banking was calculated to obtain the response for this question. The question was worded as follows:

> Now I would like you to consider the planning period for establishing the planned objectives. To what extent do you believe the managerial staff in your bank are in agreement about the planning period for establishing the planned objectives in each area?

In terms of the theoretical discussion on planning milieux (Chapter 5), the two variables AGROBJ and AGRHOR mentioned above were each dichotomized into the categories of Low and High, with the cut-off point at value 3. This enabled the formulation of the four Planning Milieux discussed in Chapter 5. Thus, to illustrate, the organization would be perceived as typified by Planning Milieu I by those subjects who believed that there was a high level of agreement (i.e., substantial or complete agreement) among organizational members about both the planning objectives and the corresponding planning horizons. Similarly, to take another instance, Planning Milieu IV would be constituted by low values (i.e., from no agreement to at best moderate agreement) for both the variables AGROBJ and AGRHOR. One notes, of course, from Figure 5.2 in the last chapter that Planning Milieux I and II are constituted by high values of the variable AGRHOR, while, similarly, Planning Milieux I and III have high values of the variable AGROBJ. This point would be relevant for the testing of Hypotheses 2 and 3 in Chapter 11.

Question 16 asked the subject to indicate what kind of decision strategies (Standardization, Negotiation, and Subjective) were used in the organization in dealing with planning matters relating to each of the five sub-areas of electronic banking. In terms of the theoretical discussions in Chapter 5, the subjects were provided with brief descriptions of the three decision modes, as follows:

> Standardization: a method which is routine -- standard procedures exist and are applicable most often.

Negotiation: a method characterized by give and take, bargaining, and negotiation.

Subjective: a method in which people often have to follow hunches/intuitions/opinions.

As the relative values were of a nominal nature, the responses for the five sub-areas were counted in terms their frequencies. Obviously, the total frequency for each subject for all the three decision modes (with acronyms STANDARD, NEGOTN, and SUBJECT) added up uniformly to a total of 5. These separate frequencies for each decision mode were then used for testing Hypotheses 5 and 6.

Question 17 elicited the sex (SEX) of the respondent, with the value 1 for males and 2 for females.

Question 18 asked for the year of birth of the subject, from which the age (AGE) was calculated.

Question 19, the last one, dealt with the educational attainment of the subject. The following educational levels were provided for appropriate indication: (1) no high school diploma, (2) high school diploma, (3) bachelor's degree, (4) master's degree, and (5) doctoral degree. It turned out that there were no respondents in the first category, and very few in the fifth. Hence, the 5 values were merged to generate three education levels (EDUCATL), namely, (1) high school diploma, (2) bachelor's degree, and (3) master's and doctoral degrees.

The questionnaire also provided some space at the very end for any comments that the subject might wish to make about the survey. Very few executives recorded any comments, and there was none of any significance for the research objectives.

RESPONSE STATISTICS

As mentioned earlier in the section on sampling, a total of 300 subjects in WESTBANK were available for distribution of the questionnaire. The number actually used was 298. Of these, after one reminder, a total of 207 usable responses were received, which works out to an overall response rate of 69.5 percent.

The distribution of the questionnaire according to the various functional areas of the WESTBANK headquarters personnel is given in Table 6.2. The functional areas are categorized by the three organizational levels of Executive & Senior Vice Presidents (ESVP), Vice Presidents (VP), and

TABLE 6.2

Responses by Functional Area and Organizational Level

Functional Area	ESVP		VP		AVP		Functional Area Total	
1. Branch Banking	(10)	4	(16)	12	(6)	3	(32)	19
2. International Banking	(8)	7	(21)	16	(19)	15	(48)	38
3. Corporate Banking	(13)	5	(11)	8	(4)	4	(28)	17
4. Financial Management	(9)	3	(10)	9	(2)	1	(21)	13
5. Credit	(2)	1	(9)	6	(3)	1	(14)	8
6. Staff Support	(5)	1	(11)	9	(12)	8	(28)	18
7. Management Services	(2)	2	(9)	7	(8)	5	(19)	14
8. Automated Data Processing	(3)	2	(36)	28	(23)	17	(62)	47
9. Planning & Marketing	(1)	1	(5)	4	(3)	2	(9)	7
10. Others (including Audit, Legal, etc.)	(10)	5	(19)	15	(8)	6	(37)	26
Organizational Level Total	(63)	31	(147)	114	(88)	62	(298)	207

Numbers in parentheses represent questionnaires sent out; other numbers indicate usable responses received.

Assistant Vice Presidents (AVP).   The   table also gives the
detailed   distribution of   the numbers   of usable   responses
received for each of the functional areas and organizational
levels.

It will be noticed from Table 6.2 that the sample of
298 subjects had 63 in the top organizational level of ESVP,
comprising 21 percent.   Similarly,   the 147 VPs and 88 AVPs
comprised 49 and   30 percent respectively of the total initial sample.   In terms of actual numbers, this was a convenience sample,   with the higher organizational   levels being
given a   greater proportional representation than   the lower
levels.   The precise percentages in the sample   out of the
total population cannot be divulged here for reasons of confidentiality,   except   to indicate that the highest levels
were included almost in their entirety, while the lower levels,   because of their large numbers,   were represented with
much lower proportions.

Thus, the proportional weightage of the highest organizational levels in the selected sample was higher in comparison   with   the   lower   levels.   This   differential
representation of the three organizational levels was delib-
erately provided for to take advantage of the availability
of the higher echelon executives who have decidedly more
important roles in the topic of this investigation.   This
also does not in any significant way affect the primary
research questions relating to individual future time perspectives and other variables.   Of course, the selection of
the subjects within each organizational level was done on a
random basis, as described earlier.

The response rates according to functional areas and
organizational levels are shown in Table 6.3.   These rates
are calculated in reference to the figures in Table 6.2.   It
will be noticed that the ESVP level response rate was 49.2
percent, which was remarkably high when one recalls the special difficulties academic researchers usually face in
obtaining the active participation of executives at the top-
most level in completing questionnaires.   The response rates
for VP and AVP levels were 77.6 and 70.5 percent respectively, giving an overall response rate of 69.5 percent.
This rate can be considered respectable for the research
population of senior executives,   and quite adequate for the
purpose of testing the research hypotheses.

It will also be noticed from Table 6.3 that the
response rates among different functional areas were uniformly at a satisfactory level, varying from the lowest 57.1
percent to the highest 79.2 percent.   These response statistics are presented merely to afford a general idea of the

TABLE 6.3

Response Rate Summary

Functional Area	N	Response Rate (%)
1. Branch Banking	19	59.4
2. International Banking	38	79.2
3. Corporate Banking	17	60.7
4. Financial Management	13	61.9
5. Credit	8	57.1
6. Staff Support	18	64.3
7. Management Services	14	73.7
8. Automated Data Processing	47	75.8
9. Planning & Marketing	7	77.8
10. Others (including Audit, Legal, etc.)	26	70.3
Total Overall	207	69.5
Executive Vice Presidents and Senior Vice Presidents (ESVP)	31	49.2
Vice Presidents (VP)	114	77.6
Assistant Vice Presidents (AVP)	62	70.5
Total Overall	207	69.5

kinds of executives in the study. The theoretical framework of the present study does not, however, propose any significance being attached to either the nature of particular functional areas or the organizational levels. Even so, as a matter of interest in organizational phenomena, some exploratory analyses will be carried out based on the organizational levels, in order to examine whether the hierarchical standing of a subject is a material factor in regard to the phenomena being researched.

RESEARCH HYPOTHESES

The hypotheses in this study are collected here for easy reference.

Hypothesis 1

Strategy makers with near future time perspective will prefer a shorter planning horizon than those with distant future time perspective.

Hypothesis 2

Strategy makers with a near future time perspective will perceive Planning Milieux I and II more than III and IV, while those with a distant future time perspective will perceive Planning Milieux III and IV more than I and II.

Hypothesis 3

Strategy makers with a near future time perspective will perceive Planning Milieux I and III more than II and IV, while those with a distant future time perspective will perceive Planning Milieux II and IV more than I and III.

Hypothesis 4

Strategy makers will perceive less agreement prevailing among organizational members concerning planning horizons than concerning planning objectives.

Hypothesis 5

> Strategy makers in Planning Milieu I will perceive the use of "standardization" decision mode more than the strategy makers in Planning Milieu IV.

Hypothesis 6

> Strategy makers in Planning Milieu IV will perceive the use of "subjective" decision mode more than the strategy makers in Planning Milieu I.

STATISTICAL METHODS

The statistical methods for analyzing and interpreting the questionnaire data need to be appropriate to the data and the research objectives. The broad objective was to explain hypothesized overall differences in preferred Planning Horizon, Agreement on Planning Objectives, and Agreement on Planning Horizons associated with Near and Distant types of Future Time Perspective. For this purpose, it was decided to use t-tests. The same method was applied to explain differences in the perception of adoption of Standardization and Subjective modes of decision making according to the specific Planning Milieu. Since all hypotheses predicted a specific direction for the results, the t-tests were based on one-tailed tests of statistical significance. The significance levels indicated in the various tables that follow were determined using an estimate of separate variance in the t-tests.

A secondary objective of the analysis was to explore how the abovementioned overall differences (related to the testing of operational hypotheses) in the aggregate sample appear in the constituent sub-samples defined by the three organizational levels. There appears to be some indication in the literature that the position of individual members in the organizational hierarchy may have some impact on their perceptions (Dearborn and Simon, 1958; Graham, 1968; Porter, 1958). This supplementary analysis was aimed at exploring whether the specific organizational level of the strategy makers made any material difference in the hypothesized associative relationships, especially as to the direction of the results. Here too, one-tailed tests were appropriate.

All statistical computations were carried out with programs from SPSS, the Statistical Package for the Social Sciences.

STATISTICAL SIGNIFICANCE: A NOTE

A test of statistical significance is relevant in the examination of the various relationships that have been predicted in terms of the operational hypotheses in this study. Additionally, there are supplementary exploratory analyses wherein such tests become necessary. When such a test of statistical significance is employed, a finding is deemed significant if it satisfies the conventionally accepted level of .05. However, as much of the spirit of this research is exploratory in nature, it was considered useful to report the near significant levels of up to .10 as well, to serve as a suggestive indicator for understanding the phenomena. This is called for in part by the arbitrarily determined cutoff levels for significance, if not also by the aggregate nature of the sample. Nevertheless, a finding is considered significant for hypothesis testing only when the degree of significance is at the commonly accepted level of .05 or better.

7
EXECUTIVE PROFILE
OF THE STUDY

DESCRIPTIVE STATISTICS FOR DISCUSSION OF RESULTS

The six chapters (8 through 13) that follow this one cover the results of the study and discussions pertaining thereto. In order to provide a basis for presenting and discussing these results, this chapter presents certain preliminary data concerning different aspects of the principal variables. These data would serve to furnish the requisite background information for appreciating the discussion attendant to hypothesis testing.

The following aspects are dealt with in the various chapters, incorporating within each chapter both the results of hypothesis testing (where appropriate) and relevant descriptive statistics:

a) Executive Profile (Chapter 7): concerned with a discussion of the different demographic characteristics of the respondents, including sex, age, education, organizational level, and job experience, and the intercorrelations among the key variables of the study.

b) Future Orientations of Executives (Chapter 8): presents data on several aspects of individual future time perspective, including the intercorrelations among the four future time subzones ("very near future," etc.) and organizational level differences.

c) Future Time Perspective and Planning Horizon (Chapter 9): examines the distribution of preferred planning horizons according to organizational level, and discusses the testing of Hypothesis 1 concerning the association of future time perspectives with preferred planning horizons.

d) Consensus on Planning Objectives and Planning Horizons (Chapter 10): presents data on perceived agreement on planning objectives and planning horizons, and discusses the testing of Hypothesis 4 relating to the differences in the level of consensus on planning objectives and planning horizons.

e) Future Time Perspective and Planning Milieux (Chapter 11): presents data on the four types of planning milieu, agreement on planning objectives, and agreement on planning horizons, and also discusses the testing of Hypotheses 2, 3, and 4, which relate to the association of individual future time perspective and the perceived consensus about planning objectives and planning horizons.

f) Planning Milieux and Modes of Decision Making (Chapter 12): discusses the distribution of the three decision making modes in terms of the planning milieux, and the testing of Hypotheses 5 and 6 dealing with the relationships between the planning milieux and the decision modes.

g) Replication at EASTBANK (Chapter 13): deals with this second sample and presents, with brief comments, the entire range of data in a format identical to that of the WESTBANK sample for ease of exposition; this chapter also discusses the comparative findings of the main study and the replication, using the same broad aspects as delineated above for explication purposes.

The principal portion of the ensuing discussion, as hitherto, will deal exclusively with the WESTBANK sample of 207 executives (Chapters 7 through 12). Chapter 13 will cover the results of the replication with the EASTBANK sample, and a comparison of the findings from the two samples.

INTERCORRELATION MATRIX OF VARIABLES

The intercorrelations among the variables utilized in this study are set out as a matrix in Table 7.1.

TABLE 7.1

Intercorrelation Matrix of all Variables

Variable	(1)ORGLEVEL	(2)FTP	(3)PLGHOR	(4)AGROBJ
(1) ORGLEVEL	1.000	.045	.039	-.094%
(2) FTP	.045	1.000	.248***	-.241***
(3) PLGHOR	.039	.248***	1.000	-.013
(4) AGROBJ	-.094%	-.241***	-.013	1.000
(5) AGRHOR	-.007	-.266***	.006	.616***
(6) STANDARD	-.111%	-.147*	-.057	.248***
(7) NEGOTN	.061	.054	-.003	-.072
(8) SUBJECT	.057	.108%	.073	-.214***

Variable	(5)AGRHOR	(6)STANDARD	(7)NEGOTN	(8)SUBJECT
(1) ORGLEVEL	.007	-.111%	.061	.057
(2) FTP	-.266***	-.147*	.054	.108%
(3) PLGHOR	.006	-.057	-.003	.073
(4) AGROBJ	.616***	.248***	-.072	-.214***
(5) AGRHOR	1.000	.157*	.017	-.218***
(6) STANDARD	.157*	1.000	-.700***	-.316***
(7) NEGOTN	.017	-.700***	1.000	-.456***
(8) SUBJECT	-.218***	-.316***	-.456***	1.000

% p<.10   * p<.05   ** p<.01   *** p<.001

Most of the significant correlations occur in relation to the future time perspective (FTP), quite in sympathy with the general theoretical thrust of this study, namely, that there are important associations between FTP and certain other variables in the strategic planning arena. The correlations of FTP with all the three key variables -- planning horizon (PLGHOR), agreement on planning objectives (AGROBJ), and agreement on planning horizon (AGRHOR) -- are significant below the .001 level.

The significant negative correlations between the three decision modes -- standardization (STANDARD), negotiation (NEGOTN), and subjective (SUBJECT) -- are only to be expected as an artifact of the question, for a respondent is required to make self-constraining choices as between them (see Question 16 of the questionnaire in Appendix A). Out of a total of 5 choices allowed, a respondent, by indicating any specific decision mode, would be reducing the permissible number of the other two, preserving the total count to a maximum of 5. This point would be clearer in a subsequent chapter, especially on a study of Table 12.1.

The rest of this chapter will mostly cover the descriptive analyses of the different demographic characteristics of the sample, including sex, age, education, organizatonal level, and length of job experience.

SEX

Some of the demographic statistics of the WESTBANK sample are given in Table 7.2, arranged according to the three organizational levels.

There were 162 males and 45 females in the final sample of 207, which works out to 21.7 percent females. However, not surprisingly, there was only one female respondent against 30 males in the ESVP category. The proportions were considerably less disparate in the VP and AVP categories, with percentages of 15.8 and 41.9 respectively.

While there were no readily available corporate sources to compare these percentages with the actual gender ratios in the organizational population, a senior executive (liaising with the author) offered the assessment that the percentages are not markedly removed from the sex distributions obtaining in the executive populations at the various corporate levels.

TABLE 7.2

Responses by Demographics and Organizational Level

Demographic Variable	ESVP	VP	AVP	Total
SEX				
Male	30 (96.8)	96 (84.2)	36 (58.1)	162 (78.3)
Female	1 (3.2)	18 (15.8)	26 (41.9)	45 (21.7)
AGE				
Upto 35 years	1 (3.2)	26 (22.8)	23 (37.1)	50 (24.2)
36 to 50 years	19 (61.3)	72 (63.2)	32 (51.6)	123 (59.4)
51 years and over	11 (35.5)	16 (14.0)	7 (11.3)	34 (16.4)
EDUCATION				
High School	2 (6.5)	29 (25.4)	26 (41.9)	57 (27.5)
Bachelor	11 (35.5)	48 (42.1)	28 (45.2)	87 (42.0)
Master+Doctor	18 (58.1)	37 (32.5)	8 (12.9)	63 (30.4)
Organizational Level Total	31	114	62	207

Numbers in parentheses represent percentages of the
frequencies within each Organizational Level.

AGE

The respondents varied in age from the lowest figure of 27 years to the highest of 64 years. When organized into three convenient groups (see Table 7.2), the age distribution of the subjects provides us with the following picture. There were 50 subjects (24.2 percent) in the category "Upto 35 years," with all except one in the VP and AVP levels. This was only to be expected, considering that the commercial banking profession ordinarily requires long years of apprenticeship at lower levels before being eligible for graduation to higher responsibilities. Arguably for the same reason, the AVPs had a relatively higher percentage in this lower age-group than the VPs (37.1 versus 22.8).

The middle age category of "36 to 50 years" was constituted by 123 subjects, or 59.4 percent of the sample. In this group, as many as 19 were in the top ESVP level, forming 61.3 percent of the 31 at that level. The 72 executives at the VP level formed a comparable 63.2 percent, while the 32 AVPs made up an expectedly lower 51.6 percent.

In the third age-group of those over 50 years, the ESVP subjects numbered 11, which works out to 35.5 of that level. In comparison, the 16 and 7 executives at the VP and AVP levels respectively constituted only 14.0 and 11.3 percent.

Overall, the age distribution in the sample seems not to be too removed from the generally expected pattern of relatively younger executives at the lower organizational levels, with older executives occupying the higher positions. The mean age of the total sample was 42.5 years, with a standard deviation of 8.4 years. The mean ages for the organizational levels were: ESVP 48.8 years, VP 42.4 years, and AVP 39.7 years.

EDUCATION

As reflected in Table 7.2, there were no subjects without at least a high school diploma. There were a total of 57 subjects with a high school diploma as their highest level of academic preparation, 87 with a bachelor's degree, 60 with a master's degree, and 3 with a doctorate. On account of the fact that there were no subjects without at least a high school diploma, and also as only 3 subjects had a doctorate, it was decided to combine the master's and doctoral levels and form a total of 3 groups to analyze the distribution of education levels in the sample (see Table 7.2).

The group of 57 with high school diplomas was made up of only 2 at the ESVP level, and 29 and 26 at the VP and AVP levels respectively. The percentages of subjects at this lowest education category for each organizational level were 6.5 (ESVP), 25.4 (VP), and 41.9 (AVP). The corresponding percentages for the middle education category of bachelor's degree holders were 35.5, 42.1, and 45.2. These figures indicate that perhaps promotions for higher positions, in so far as WESTBANK was concerned, had some relationship with attainments in higher education. The third highest education category distribution would seem to indicate this organizational characteristic even more plainly. The percentages, in identical order, were 58.1, 32.5, and 12.9.

As a general comment, one would probably be justified in observing that the level of education seems to have a significant association with the organizational level of the subject, with higher educational attainments tending to go with upper hierarchical levels in this bank.

Perhaps of some interest too is the fact that as much as 27.5 percent of the executives had only a high school education. It may be of interest to explore the comparative data in various other banks and other industries to see whether this is specific to the organization studied or is characteristic of the commercial banking industry.

ORGANIZATIONAL LEVEL

As explained earlier, owing to the small number of subjects at the level of Executive Vice President, it was considered desirable to combine this corporate title with that of Senior Vice President to constitute the ESVP level. The sample in the study thus had 31 members at the ESVP level, 114 at the VP level, and 62 at the AVP level, comprising, respectively, 15.0 percent, 55.1 percent, and 30.0 percent of the 207 subjects. The detailed demographic characteristics of the three levels have already been discussed in the earlier sections.

JOB EXPERIENCE

The length of time that the executives in the sample worked in the bank, or job experience (JOBEXP), is shown in Table 7.3. The mean job experience was 17.42 years for the ESVP level, 13.43 years for the VP level, and 10.26 years for the AVP level. The respective medians were 17.25,

TABLE 7.3

Job Experience and Organizational Level

Job Experience	ESVP	VP	AVP	Total
Upto 5 years	6 (19.4)	25 (21.9)	23 (37.1)	54 (26.1)
6 - 10 years	3 (9.7)	22 (19.3)	9 (14.5)	34 (16.4)
11 - 15 years	4 (12.9)	24 (21.1)	19 (30.6)	47 (22.7)
16 - 20 years	5 (16.1)	21 (18.4)	5 (8.1)	31 (15.0)
21 - 25 years	8 (25.8)	12 (10.5)	2 (3.2)	22 (10.6)
26 plus years	5 (16.1)	10 (8.8)	4 (6.5)	19 (9.2)
Total	31 (100.0)	114 (100.0)	62 (100.0)	207 (100.0)
Mean	17.42	13.43	10.26	13.08
S.D.	10.15	8.27	7.60	8.66

Numbers in parentheses represent percentages of the
frequencies within each Organizational Level.

12.30, and 10.17 years. For the sample as a whole, the mean and median were 13.08 and 11.67 years, with values ranging from the lowest 1 year to the highest 46 years.

The job experience of the subjects was categorized into six convenient groups at 5-year intervals, with the last group being those above 25 years (and upto 46 years). As is to be expected, a greater percentage of executives at the ESVP level had longer job experience compared to the other two levels. For instance, those with more than 15 years in the bank constituted as much as 58.0 percent at the ESVP level, compared to only 37.7 percent and 17.8 percent at the VP and AVP levels. The contrast was even more if we considered, for example, job experience of over 20 years: the corresponding percentages were 41.1 vis-a-vis 19.3 and 9.7. It is to be noted, though, that at each of the three levels there exists a fair degree of variation in the length of experience, as evidenced by the large standard deviations. This perhaps points to the fact that unlike, say, the defense services, where career progression is substantially in tandem with length of service, a large commercial bank would have both new executives inducted from outside the organization and accelerated advancement based on performance.

8
ANALYSIS OF
FUTURE ORIENTATIONS

ANALYSIS OF FOUR FUTURE SUBZONES

The distribution of the variable FTP (individual future time perspective) among the strategy makers is examined in this chapter. There are, it will be recalled, four subzones in the future time dimension, and the respective variables are FTPVNEAR ("very near future"), FTPNEAR ("near future"), FTPDIST ("distant future"), and FTPVDIST ("very distant future"). The variable FTP of course denotes the mean score of a strategy maker, computed by averaging the frequencies of events in the four subzones. The correlations among the overall FTP and the four subzone variables are given in Table 8.1.

It will be noticed that there are a large number of significant correlations. This is unremarkable in itself, for the mean score of FTP is a derivative of the four subzone variables. Furthermore, the direction of relationships among the four subzone variables is an artifact of the requirement that the respondent is restricted to nine events, which means that the more events are mentioned in one subzone the less is available in the others.

There are, however, a few points worth noting about the data in Table 8.1. First, the FTP score is negatively related to the two "near-type" subzones and positively related to the two "distant-type" subzones. Thus, as a general observation, the strategy makers as a group had a future time perspective which was somewhere between what they considered as near future and distant future. Second, each subzone was negatively related to all the others, mostly at significant levels. This points toward a certain

TABLE 8.1

Intercorrelation Matrix of all FTP Variables

Variable	(1) FTP	(2) FTPVNEAR	(3) FTPNEAR	(4) FTPDIST	(5) FTPVDIST
(1) FTP	1.000	-.771***	-.481***	.574***	.705***
(2) FTPVNEAR	-.771***	1.000	-.118%	-.504***	-.270***
(3) FTPNEAR	-.481***	-.118%	1.000	-.550***	-.423***
(4) FTPDIST	.574***	-.504***	-.550***	1.000	-.098%
(5) FTPVDIST	.705***	-.270***	-.423***	-.098%	1.000

% p<.10   * p<.05   ** p<.01   *** p<.001

degree of differentiation of the subzones among the strategy makers.

Third, the two near-type subzones are not significantly associated with each other. The same holds true for the two distant-type subzones. This could be an indication that on an overall basis the strategy makers did not distinguish too specifically the two contiguous near-type subzones, and so also the two distant-type subzones. However, the strategy makers did differentiate very clearly the broad "near" and "distant" segments as between themselves. Finally, it needs to be noted that while the directions of the correlations in Table 8.1 are determined in the main by the computing process, some of the relationships are fairly weak in value, suggesting that not all of the outcomes are completely arti-factual in nature.

Irrespective, however, of the reasons for the various associations among the variables, there is a reasonably wide dispersion of frequencies of events among the four subzones, as displayed in Table 8.2.

TABLE 8.2

Percentages of Events in Four Future Time Subzones

Number of Events	Very Near	Near	Distant	Very Distant
0	15.3	1.1	4.5	29.4
1	37.9	7.3	7.3	35.0
2	29.9	15.8	33.3	23.7
3	11.9	31.6	26.0	10.2
4	3.4	27.7	16.4	1.1
5	0.0	11.9	6.8	0.6
6	1.1	2.3	5.1	0.0
7	0.6	0.6	0.0	0.0
8	0.0	1.7	0.0	0.0
9	0.0	0.0	0.6	0.0
Total	279	593	508	213
Mean	1.58	3.35	2.87	1.20
S.D.	1.18	1.38	1.46	1.05

The figures for Total, Mean, and S.D. indicate the number of events in each future time subzone.

An examination of the frequency distribution percentages shows that a vast majority of the strategic actors have indicated their dominant life events in most of the four subzones, as very few have anticipated all or a disproportionately large number of events in any one subzone. It will be noticed that the total number of events reported in the four subzones are 279, 593, 508, and 213, which aggregates to 1593. This number is equal to nine times the number of respondents (177). (It should be noted here that the remaining 30 respondents, out of the total of 207 who furnished usable questionnaires, failed to complete the item relating to the variable FTP.)

If the distribution of events were a result of random frequencies, it would have resulted in each subzone attracting 2.25 events per subject. In actuality, though, there were wide variations. For instance, 29 percent of the strategy makers have failed to place any event in the "very distant" future time subzone. For these subjects, it appears the life space does not extend to that subzone. Another 35 percent of the respondents anticipate only one event in that subzone. Thus over 64 percent of the sample have none or only one event in the "very distant" subzone. The "very near" future subzone appears to be similarly wanting, with 53 percent of the subjects mentioning none or only one event in that subzone.

A look at the means of the different subzones shows that the number of events in the "near" subzone (3.35) is substantially higher than those of the "very near" and "very distant" subzones, with "distant" subzone being the second most populous (2.87 events). Thus the two middle subzones are predominant in terms of the number of anticipated important events in the future life space of the respondents.

SCORING AND ANALYSIS OF FUTURE TIME PERSPECTIVE

The scoring procedure for determining the future time perspective (FTP value) of individual strategy makers was indicated in the last chapter. Briefly, this was the average value of the nine events, with a value of 1 being assigned to an event in the "very near" subzone, and a value of 4 for an event in the "very distant" subzone, with the intermediate values of 2 and 3 for the other two subzones. Obviously, an FTP score representing a point midway between the "near" and "distant" future time subzones would be expected in case future time perspectives were not associated with any individual differences. In other words, if

TABLE 8.3

Future Time Perspective and Organizational Level

FTP	ESVP	VP	AVP	Total
0.00 - 2.00	5 (20.8)	15 (15.8)	10 (17.2)	30 (16.9)
2.00 - 2.25	1 (4.2)	17 (17.9)	11 (19.0)	29 (16.4)
2.25 - 2.50	1 (4.2)	29 (30.5)	13 (22.4)	43 (24.3)
2.50 - 2.75	12 (50.0)	17 (17.9)	10 (17.2)	39 (22.0)
2.75 plus	5 (20.8)	17 (17.9)	14 (24.1)	36 (20.3)
Total	24 (100.0)	95 (100.0)	58 (100.0)	177 (100.0)
Mean	2.50	2.39	2.42	2.41
S.D.	0.37	0.34	0.38	0.36

Numbers in parentheses represent percentages of the frequencies within each Organizational Level.

the future time perspectives were a random phenomenon, we would obtain 2.5 as the FTP mean score for the total sample.

Table 8.3 displays the various FTP scores according to the organizational levels of the strategy makers. As mentioned earlier, although organizational level differences are not central to this study, the data would be analyzed for these differences in order to afford a clearer picture of the overall distribution of temporal perspectives of the

TABLE 8.4

FTP Variables and Organizational Level

Variable	ESVP (1)	VP (2)	AVP (3)	Significance Level of T-Tests		
				1:2	1:3	2:3
FTP	2.500	2.386	2.416	n.s.	n.s.	n.s.
N	24	95	58			
FTPVNEAR	1.250	1.568	1.724	n.s.	.072	n.s.
N	24	95	58			
FTPNEAR	3.250	3.495	3.155	n.s.	n.s.	n.s.
N	24	95	58			
FTPDIST	3.250	2.832	2.776	n.s.	n.s.	n.s.
N	24	95	58			
FTPVDIST	1.250	1.105	1.345	n.s.	n.s.	n.s.
N	24	95	58			

Significance levels were determined on the basis of
two-tailed t-tests using an estimate of separate variance.
(Note that the aggregate of the four future time subzones
add up to 9 for each Organizational Level.)

strategy makers. The mean FTP is 2.41 for all the reporting
subjects, which denotes a point nearer to the "near" subzone
than the "distant" subzone. The FTP values for the strategy
makers in the three organizational levels are more or less
the same, with those relating to the VPs and AVPs being
close to each other (2.39 and 2.42) in comparison with that
of the ESVPs (2.50). However, when FTP values are examined
by arranging them in five convenient slices, each of which
seems to attract around 20 percent of the total sample, it
seems that a higher percentage of ESVP level strategic
actors (71 percent) have FTP values above 2.50, as compared

to 36 percent for VPs and 41 percent for AVPs.   The dispersion of subjects is most even for the AVP group in the five
FTP slices, and most uneven in the case of the ESVPs.

In order to further examine the organizational level
differences of various future time perspective variables
(the overall mean FTP and the four subzones), an analysis is
presented in Table 8.4.   It is clear that there are no significant statistical differences in any of the five variables as between the three categories of strategy makers.

As there appears to be no research data on future time
perspective of top executives in the business world, the
results of this table are of some interest.   It is clear
from the analysis that there are no discernible,   direct
organizational level effect on the FTP values of individual
strategy makers.   It is all the more remarkable that the
lack of statistically significant differences between the
three organizational levels is consistent for each of the
four subzones considered separately.   To a certain extent,
this lends credence to the contention of this author, based
on his extensive observations as a practicing executive,
that the higher echelons of corporate hierarchies do not
necessarily harbor incumbents with decidedly more prominent
future orientations.

9
FUTURE ORIENTATIONS
AND PLANNING HORIZONS

ANALYSIS OF PLANNING HORIZONS

Table 9.1 displays the distribution of the variable PLGHOR (preferred planning horizon) based on the responses to Question 10 of the survey questionnaire (see Appendix A).

Eight convenient slices of the planning horizon values are arranged for each of the three organizational levels. The table shows that 20.5 percent of the strategy makers preferred a planning horizon of 2.5 to 3 years, which was the highest percentage for any particular PLGHOR slice. The next highest (at 17.9 percent) related to the adjacent slice of 2 to 2.5 years. These two slices (i.e., planning horizon of over 2 years and upto 3 years) accounted for over 48 percent of the AVPs, 35.5 percent of the VPs, and 28 percent of the ESVPs. A tendency towards the higher slices is discernible for the VP group, with the slices of over 3 years accounting for 47 percent, in comparison with the corresponding percentages of 9 and 15 for ESVPs and AVPs.

The mean value of PLGHOR for the strategy makers as a whole came to 2.85 years. The respective mean values for the three organizational levels are not too different from each other (2.75, 2.90, and 2.83 years). This indicates that there is not much of a difference in the preferences for planning horizons among the strategy makers at the three organizational levels. This finding, incidentally, has the same flavor as that relating to the absence of differences in the mean FTP values at the three organizational levels discussed in the preceding chapter. The interesting question as to whether this absence of organizational level differentiation is also true for the association between FTP

117

TABLE 9.1

Preferred Planning Horizons and Organizational Level

PLGHOR	ESVP	VP	AVP	Total
0.0 - 1.0 year	2 (8.0)	4 (3.6)	3 (5.0)	9 (4.6)
1.0 - 1.5 years	2 (8.0)	6 (5.5)	4 (6.7)	12 (6.2)
1.5 - 2.0 years	5 (20.0)	14 (12.7)	9 (15.0)	28 (14.4)
2.0 - 2.5 years	3 (12.0)	20 (18.2)	12 (20.0)	35 (17.9)
2.5 - 3.0 years	4 (16.0)	19 (17.3)	17 (28.3)	40 (20.5)
3.0 - 3.5 years	1 (4.0)	20 (18.2)	7 (11.7)	28 (14.4)
3.5 - 4.0 years	4 (16.0)	13 (11.8)	3 (5.0)	20 (10.3)
4.0 plus years	4 (16.0)	14 (12.7)	5 (8.3)	23 (11.8)
Total	25 (100.0)	110 (100.0)	60 (100.0)	195 (100.0)
Mean	2.83	2.90	2.75	2.85
S.D.	1.29	1.04	1.12	1.09

Numbers in parentheses represent percentages of the frequencies within each Organizational Level.

and PLGHOR will be examined presently within the rubric of Hypothesis 1 of this study.

NEAR AND DISTANT FUTURE TIME PERSPECTIVE

The testing of various hypotheses (including Hypothesis 1 in this chapter) relating to the future time perspective (FTP), called for the creation of a new variable. This derived variable, termed FTPND, was created by taking the lowest and highest thirds of the range of FTP values. These extreme thirds were utilized for comparison purposes, and were designated as "Near" and "Distant" categories respectively of the future time perspective. On an examination of the distribution of values of FTP (as reflected in Table 9.1), it appeared appropriate to select the cut-off points of 2.40 and 2.60, which were 0.10 on either side of the midpoint (2.50) of FTP values (1 to 4). The actual values ranged between 1.33 and 3.11.

This trichotomizing of the FTP values resulted in 79 respondents in the group termed as Near FTP, and 49 respondents in the group designated as Distant FTP. The actual numbers in the Near and Distant categories of the FTPND variable would be a few subjects less in the analyses that follow on account of the pairwise deletion of missing values in the SPSS statistical programs used.

RELATIONSHIP BETWEEN FUTURE TIME PERSPECTIVE AND PLANNING HORIZON

In terms of Hypothesis 1, strategy makers with near future time perspective will prefer a shorter planning horizon than those with distant future time perspective. To use the variable acronyms, the hypothesis translates to the expectation that Near FTP group would have a significantly lower PLGHOR value than the Distant FTP group. The analysis for testing the hypothesis was done using the t-test. Since the hypothesis predicts a specific direction, one-tailed tests of statistical significance were employed, both for the overall sample and for the three organizational levels. As evident from Table 9.2, Hypothesis 1 was confirmed at the p < .001 level of significance.

It will be observed from the table that the preferred planning horizon of Near FTP strategy makers was slightly less than two and a half years. The relevant figure for the strategy makers with Distant FTP was very near three years.

TABLE 9.2

Planning Horizons Based on Near vs Distant FTP

| | Preferred Planning Horizon | | Significance |
	Near FTP	Distant FTP	Level of T-Tests
OVERALL	2.476	2.996	.001
N	75	45	
ORGANIZATIONAL LEVEL			
ESVP	2.580	3.171	n.s.
N	5	7	
VP	2.560	3.057	.018
N	48	23	
AVP	2.268	2.820	.032
N	22	15	

The direction of longer planning horizons for more distant future time perspectives held consistently for all the three organizational levels, although the results were not statistically significant for the ESVPs.

The mean value of planning horizon preferences (PLGHOR) for the sample was 2.85 years. The preferred planning horizons of the two FTP groups may not seem to differ to a substantial degree in absolute terms. The comparatively small difference in the PLGHOR values may or may not have important operational ramifications.

We are not concerned with the absolute values of preferred planning horizons in this study. The hypothesis under examination deals with the question as to whether the planning horizon preferences of individual strategy makers are associated with their future time perspectives.

It is entirely possible that the PLGHOR values would vary over time, with the type of business, nature of the industry, size of the organization, etc. Take note, though, that the hypothesis relates expressly to a specified and shared strategy making arena. Once the organizational context changes, the absolute PLGHOR values would be expected to alter also.

The confirmed hypothesis provides the necessary rationale for exploring more refined ways in which strategy makers with widely differing FTP scores could be identified. This should make it possible to assign different strategy makers to activities with different planning horizons, based on individual future time perspectives. Such selective assignments would, needless to say, be permissible only if one overcomes the extant presumption that executives do not need to be distinguished in terms of their individual future orientations. A related, and similarly deleterious, presumption is that all executives are able to attend to various kinds of planning activities with equal facility.

RELATIONSHIP BETWEEN SHORT/LONG PLANNING HORIZONS AND FUTURE TIME PERSPECTIVE

The association between the future time perspective of individuals and their preference for planning horizons was the main thrust of the hypothesis testing thus far in this chapter. This association was explored only in one direction, namely, the planning horizon preferences were found on the basis of given FTP values. A further exploratory analysis was undertaken to find out whether the expected association was also true in the reverse direction. The question now is whether the subjects with shorter planning horizon preferences were the ones with lower values of FTP. And complementarily, whether the longer planning horizon preferences were associated with higher FTP values. If these relationships held true, as one would reasonably expect, then the hypothesized association of FTP and PLGHOR could be considered a fairly tight bonding.

As a preliminary for testing this complementary phenomenon, it was necessary to create a new variable, this with the acronym PLGHORSL, by trichotomizing the PLGHOR values (range 0.50 year to 6.40 years; median 2.76 years), and including the lowest and highest thirds for comparison purposes. These extreme thirds were designated as "Short" and "Long" categories respectively of the preferred planning horizons. The distribution of values of PLGHOR (as reflected in Table 9.1) suggested the convenient cut-off points of 2 years and 3 years.

TABLE 9.3

FTP Based on Short vs Long Planning Horizon

| | Future Time Perspective | | Significance |
	Short Plg Hor	Long Plg Hor	Level of T-Tests
OVERALL	2.252	2.504	.001
N	45	56	
ORGANIZATIONAL LEVEL			
ESVP	2.236	2.556	.048
N	8	6	
VP	2.222	2.469	.010
N	21	36	
AVP	2.299	2.571	.017
N	16	14	

This trichotomizing of the PLGHOR values resulted in 49 subjects in the group with preference for a short planning horizon (with PLGHOR values of 2 years or less). Similarly, 71 subjects fell into the group which preferred a long planning horizon (with PLGHOR values of over 3 years). The actual numbers in the analysis reflect a few subjects less in both the Short and Long categories of PLGHORSL owing to the pairwise deletion of missing values.

Table 9.3 sets out the results of the exploratory analysis mentioned above. The Short PLGHOR strategy makers do indeed appear to have a significantly lower FTP than those with Long PLGHOR (significant at the p < .001 level). The detailed analysis at the three organizational levels also demonstrate the same direction of difference at statistically significant levels.

As discussed earlier, the confirmation of this reverse relationship helps cement the linkage between the future

time perspective of individuals and their preferences for
shorter or longer planning horizons. This finding provides
us with sufficient rationale for exploring further the role
of the new construct of individual future orientations in
the strategy making process.

10
CONSENSUS ON PLANNING
OBJECTIVES AND PLANNING HORIZONS

Basically, the direction of planning is consensual. Problems occur not only in the area of objectives but also with the time frame of that direction. The successful implementation of a strategic plan is thus dependent significantly upon a consensus among organizational members about corporate planning objectives and planning horizons. While the means of achieving such a consensus are often the subject of research and practice, such as in the decision making literature, it seems also necessary to ascertain what degree of consensus typically obtains in organizations in the highest echelons. At a minimum, a perception of consensus on planning objectives and planning horizons is critical for an individual's efforts at plan implementation.

It will be recalled from Chapter 5 that, in terms of Hypothesis 4, the consensus level would be less for planning horizons than for planning objectives. It was also suggested that the degree of perceived consensus among organizational members regarding planning objectives and planning horizons would be less than substantial and far from complete. These contentions were empirically investigated, with data relating to the overall sample as well as separately for the three levels of organizational positions.

PERCEPTION OF CONSENSUS

The critical role of individual perceptions in organizational decision making has been acknowledged in the planning literature. The need for further studies of the perceptions and world views of managers has also received emphasis in recent years (see Chapter 2). In the area of plan implementation, it becomes particularly crucial for organizations to insure that a sufficiently high degree of at-large consensus is perceived by all concerned.

Specifically, it is essential that strategic actors perceive, as a precondition for energetic action, that a consensus about planning objectives exists among all organizational members. Curiously, though, despite the recognition that the perception of consensus impinges substantively on strategy implementation (as indeed various other organizational processes also), researchers have with few exceptions tended to stay away from investigating this aspect. However, Bourgeois (1980a) carried out an exploratory study assessing the relationship between consensus among top management teams and economic performance in 12 corporations. Even in this case, however, the notion of consensus is that of straightforward agreement among participants, and not an individual member's perception of prevailing consensus among the body of senior managerial staff.

The distinct advantages of a shared perception of consensus on planning objectives have, of course, been noted by researchers, although empirical investigations have rarely been carried out. Tilles (1963:121), for instance, mentions the following among criteria for strategic success: "the degree of consensus which exists among executives concerning corporate goals and policies." In a similar vein, Child (1974:8) notes that "the more agreement there is among senior managers as to which objectives have priority, the more successful the organization will be in attaining them." The point that needs to be emphasized here, though, is that individual perceptions of organizational members about that desired consensus is what is critical. In this chapter, we shall seek to empirically assess that critical phenomenon of perceived consensus.

It is easy to see that there is an inordinately wide scope for diminished levels of perceived consensus. To quote Goodman and Huff (1978:336): "A set of perceivers, each with his own image of the world, data sources, and valuation, may hold not only different but incompatible appreciations of the same phenomenon, none of which can be called the best." Hence, it is unlikely that a strategic actor will perceive that there is complete consensus about corporate planning objectives among people in an organization.

On the basis of the above discussion, it would be reasonable to expect that the degree of consensus perceived by strategy makers regarding both planning objectives and plan-

TABLE 10.1

Agreement on Planning Objectives and Organizational Level

AGROBJ	ESVP	VP	AVP	Total
No agreement	0 (0.0)	0 (0.0)	0 (0.0)	0 (0.0)
Very little agreement	3 (10.0)	11 (9.7)	5 (8.1)	19 (9.3)
Moderate agreement	13 (43.3)	58 (51.3)	23 (37.1)	94 (45.9)
Substantial agreement	11 (36.7)	41 (36.3)	26 (41.9)	78 (38.0)
Complete agreement	3 (10.0)	3 (2.7)	8 (12.9)	14 (6.8)
Total	30 (100.0)	113 (100.0)	62 (100.0)	205 (100.0)
Mean S.D.	3.47 0.82	3.32 0.69	3.60 0.82	3.42 0.75

Numbers in parentheses represent percentages of the
frequencies within each Organizational Level.

ning horizons would be somewhat less than substantial or complete. We shall now analyze the survey data to see whether this expectation is valid. Later, we shall test Hypothesis 4 regarding differential consensus on planning objectives and planning horizons.

ANALYSIS OF AGREEMENT ON PLANNING OBJECTIVES

Table 10.1 displays the distribution of perceived degree of agreement among organizational members regarding planning objectives.

It is evident from the table that 114 (or over 55 percent) of the 205 responding subjects believed that very little or moderate agreement existed, while 92 (or nearly 45 percent) thought that there was substantial or complete agreement about planning objectives. Notice that no strategy maker perceived a total lack of agreement.

No particularly wild variations are discernible in the percentages in different agreement categories when individual organizational levels are scrutinized. The same consistency is evident in the mean agreement values among the three organizational groups of strategy makers. The overall mean was 3.42, which indicates a point closer to the moderate agreement level than the substantial agreement category. This confirms the earlier contention that the degree of consensus perceived by strategy makers regarding planning objectives would be less than substantial or complete.

ANALYSIS OF AGREEMENT ON PLANNING HORIZONS

Turning to the other variable, Table 10.2 gives the distribution of the perceived degree of agreement among organizational members regarding an appropriate planning horizon. The table shows that only about 33 percent of the 204 responding subjects consider that there was a high level of agreement concerning the planning horizon.

Here too, as for the agreement on planning objectives, the individual organizational level data suggest no violent deviations in the organizational level figures as compared with the percentage for the overall sample. The only exception worth mentioning is that in respect of proportions relating to the "complete agreement" category, the three organizational levels differed somewhat as between the ESVPs (10.3 percent) and AVPs (9.7 percent) on the one hand, and the VPs (only 1.8 percent) and the overall sample (5.4 per-

TABLE 10.2

Agreement on Planning Horizons and Organizational Level

AGRHOR	ESVP	VP	AVP	Total
No agreement	0 (0.0)	2 (1.8)	0 (0.0)	2 (1.0)
Very little agreement	3 (10.3)	18 (15.9)	8 (12.9)	29 (14.2)
Moderate agreement	16 (55.2)	56 (49.6)	34 (54.8)	106 (52.0)
Substantial agreement	7 (24.1)	35 (31.0)	14 (22.6)	56 (27.5)
Complete agreement	3 (10.3)	2 (1.8)	6 (9.7)	11 (5.4)
Total	29 (100.0)	113 (100.0)	62 (100.0)	204 (100.0)
Mean	3.35	3.15	3.29	3.22
S.D.	0.81	0.77	0.82	0.79

Numbers in parentheses represent percentages of the
frequencies within each Organizational Level.

TABLE 10.3

Agreement on Planning Objectives and Planning Horizons

	Agreement on		Significance
	Plg Objectives	Plg Horizons	Level of T-Tests
OVERALL	3.427	3.221	.001
N	204	204	
ORGANIZATIONAL LEVEL			
ESVP	3.483	3.345	.052
N	29	29	
VP	3.319	3.150	.007
N	113	113	
AVP	3.597	3.290	.001
N	62	62	

cent) on the other. A certain consistency is also noticeable for the means of the three organizational levels. The
overall mean was 3.22, which is closer to the moderate
agreement level than the substantial agreement category.
This bears out the expectation that the degree of consensus
perceived by strategy makers regarding planning horizons
would be less than substantial or complete.

COMPARING DEGREES OF PERCEIVED CONSENSUS ABOUT
PLANNING OBJECTIVES AND PLANNING HORIZONS

In terms of Hypothesis 4, strategy makers would perceive less agreement prevailing among organizational members
concerning planning horizons than concerning planning objectives. This was predicted on the basis of the reasoning
that there is generally less importance bestowed on planning

horizon in the business world, and a strategy maker would be likely to perceive less consensus obtaining among organizational members arising out of this relative inattention and lack of awareness.

Table 10.3 displays the results of the analysis comparing the means of the variables AGROBJ and AGRHOR.   The hypothesis was confirmed at the p < .001 level of significance with a one-tailed t-test.   The relative organizational level tests also provided a similar confirmation, except that the significance for the ESVP group was slightly outside the conventional .05 level.   The conclusion is that a higher level of agreement is generally perceived by strategy makers in the case of planning objectives in comparison with planning horizons.

The managerial implications of the relatively significant lack of consensus on planning objectives and planning horizons will be discussed in Chapter 15.

11
FUTURE ORIENTATIONS
AND PLANNING MILIEUX

ANALYSIS OF FOUR PLANNING MILIEUX

It will be recalled from Chapter 5 that the four Planning Milieux were formulated by dichotomizing the values of the two variables AGROBJ (perceived agreement on planning objectives) and AGRHOR (perceived agreement on planning horizons), and combining them to produce a typology in the form of a two-by-two matrix. Thus, for instance, Planning Milieu I would be perceived by those strategy makers who believed that a high degree of agreement existed among organizational members about both the planning objectives in electronic banking and the appropriate planning horizons.

Before proceeding to test Hypotheses 2 and 3, it would be helpful to gain a general idea about the distribution of subjects in the various planning milieux. Table 11.1 sets out the relevant information. Of the 204 subjects reporting on both the constituent variables, almost half (48 percent) perceived that the planning milieu was of type IV, or that there was relatively low agreement generally among the organizational members about both planning objectives and planning horizons. Noteworthy too is the finding that slightly over a quarter (26 percent) of the strategy makers believed in the contrary situation, in which there was a relatively high level of agreement among organizational members on both planning objectives and planning horizons (Planning Milieu I).

Not entirely unexpectedly, the number of strategy makers perceiving one or the other of the two "mixed" planning milieux (II and III) was relatively small, accounting for only 26 percent between them. Nevertheless, it is to be

TABLE 11.1

Frequencies of Planning Milieux

	Planning Milieu			
	I	II	III	IV
OVERALL	53 (26.0)	14 (6.9)	39 (19.1)	98 (48.0)
ORGANIZATIONAL LEVEL				
ESVP	9 (31.0)	1 (3.4)	5 (17.2)	14 (48.3)
VP	26 (23.0)	11 (9.7)	18 (15.9)	58 (51.3)
AVP	18 (29.0)	2 (3.2)	16 (25.8)	26 (41.9)

Numbers in parantheses represent percentages of the
frequencies within each Organizational Level.

noted that more strategy makers perceived low agreement for
planning horizons than for planning objectives, so that
Planning Milieu III had 19.1 percent of the subjects as
against only 6.9 percent in Planning Milieu II.

A remarkable finding is that the proportionate distribution of strategy makers among the four planning milieux
follows more or less the same pattern in the case of all the
three organizational levels. This should not be too sur-
prising, though, if the thrust of Hypotheses 2 and 3 is
remembered. The perceptions of planning milieux have been
predicated therein as being associated with future time perspective rather than with organizational level.

RELATIONSHIP BETWEEN FUTURE TIME PERSPECTIVE
AND AGREEMENT ON PLANNING OBJECTIVES

Hypothesis 3 states that strategy makers with a near future time perspective will perceive Planning Milieux I and III more than II and IV, while those with a distant future time perspective will perceive Planning Milieux II and IV more than I and III. One notes, of course, that Planning Milieux I and III have high values of the variable AGROBJ, and that, complementarily, low values of the variable serve to constitute Planning Milieux II and IV (see Figure 5.2).

The hypothesis translates to a prediction that the Near FTP strategy makers will be associated with a higher AGROBJ (a high level of agreement on planning objectives, which connotes Planning Milieux I and III) compared to the Distant FTP strategy makers.

The results of a one-tailed t-test are set out in Table 11.2. The hypothesis was confirmed at the $p < .002$ level of significance. This confirmation also holds true for each of the three organizational levels.

RELATIONSHIP BETWEEN FUTURE TIME PERSPECTIVE
AND AGREEMENT ON PLANNING HORIZONS

Hypothesis 2 states that strategy makers with a near future time perspective will perceive Planning Milieux I and II more than III and IV, while those with a distant future time perspective will perceive Planning Milieux III and IV more than I and II. It will be recalled that the high values of the variable AGRHOR serve to constitute Planning Milieux I and II, and the low ones III and IV (represented graphically in Figure 5.2).

The hypothesis translates to a prediction that the Near FTP strategy makers will be associated with a higher AGRHOR (a high level of agreement on planning horizons, which connotes Planning Milieux I and II) in comparison with the Distant FTP strategy makers.

The results of the one-tailed t-test are given in Table 11.3. The hypothesis was confirmed at the $p < .001$ level of significance. This confirmation also holds for each of the three organizational levels.

TABLE 11.2

Agreement on Planning Objectives Based on FTP

	Agreement on Planning Objectives		Significance Level of T-Tests
	Near FTP	Distant FTP	
OVERALL	3.494	3.125	.002
N	79	48	
ORGANIZATIONAL LEVEL			
ESVP	4.000	3.100	.032
N	6	10	
VP	3.360	3.046	.038
N	50	22	
AVP	3.652	3.250	.030
N	23	16	

RELATIONSHIP BETWEEN PLANNING MILIEUX
AND FUTURE TIME PERSPECTIVE

The foregoing two hypotheses in this chapter have been concerned with the association of time perspective and the nature of the perceived planning milieux. The results clearly indicate that a strategy maker with a Near FTP would perceive more agreement prevailing among organizational members, both about planning objectives and planning horizons, when compared with the strategy maker with a Distant FTP.

It follows that the Near FTP subjects would be more likely to perceive Planning Milieu I than Planning Milieu IV (these two planning milieux are the common ones in Hypotheses 2 and 3). It seems worthwhile, therefore, to explore whether this association of FTP and the two planning milieux (I and IV) is also true, as one would expect, in the reverse direction, namely, that subjects placing themselves

TABLE 11.3

Agreement on Planning Horizons Based on FTP

| | Agreement on Planning Horizons | | Significance |
	Near FTP	Distant FTP	Level of T-Tests
OVERALL	3.417	2.979	.001
N	79	48	
ORGANIZATIONAL LEVEL			
ESVP	4.000	3.100	.032
N	6	10	
VP	3.320	2.864	.019
N	50	22	
AVP	3.478	3.063	.022
N	23	16	

in Planning Milieu I have an FTP value significantly lower than subjects in Planning Milieu IV.

Table 11.4 gives the results of the analysis for the subjects overall and in terms of organizational levels. As will be observed, the subjects in Planning Milieu I do indeed have a significantly lower FTP compared to those belonging to Planning Milieu IV (significant at p < .001 level). The organizational level data also are significant in the expected direction.

These results seem to lend credence to the idea put forward earlier (see Chapter 5), namely, that the "near future" oriented person would be likely to "telescope" the potential future onto a smaller canvass than would a "distant future" person. The scope for perceived differences among organizational members would seem to be less for the "near future" type of strategy maker, as all the potentiality of the future would be condensed into a smaller time-

TABLE 11.4

Future Time Perspective in Planning Milieux I and IV

| | Future Time Perspective | | Significance |
	Plg Mil I	Plg Mil IV	Level of T-Tests
OVERALL	2.225	2.498	.001
N	46	85	
ORGANIZATIONAL LEVEL			
ESVP	2.389	2.771	.029
N	8	10	
VP	2.222	2.467	.002
N	22	50	
AVP	2.146	2.476	.003
N	16	25	

space field. This perceptually heightened density of a "short-spread" future (Near FTP) connotes a reduced opportunity for widely varying opinions among organizational members.

Conversely, the Distant FTP person, perceiving a much more extended, "long-spread," attenuated future, has less of a compulsion to posit a forced concentration of closely-resembling opinions among organizational members.   To such a person, there is a relatively generous time-space field in which various and varying opinions could, and hence also would, have their full play.   Which of course translates to less perceived agreement among organizational members.

This interpretation of the possible mechanism that guides the strategy maker in perceiving more or less consensus among organizational members can only be termed as tentative in nature.   In empirical terms, though, we have seen in the last chapter that at best only a moderate level of consensus is perceived overall, and that consensus of planning horizons is rated lower than that on planning objectives. The question seems interesting enough to warrant further research. Meanwhile, suffice it to say that the foregoing two empirically confirmed hypotheses would appear to be eminently hospitable to that interpretation.

The implications of the results for managerial practice are particularly significant in the implementation of strategic plans. Without a common consensus among the general body of organizational members about what is perceived as planning objectives and planning horizons, it would be difficult to ensure proper motivation and effort to work toward a shared strategic direction. Performance evaluation would also be difficult to carry out in such a situation. Some further managerial implications will be discussed in the concluding chapter.

12

PLANNING MILIEUX
AND MODES OF DECISION MAKING

In this chapter, the relationships between perceived planning milieux and the perceived decision making modes will be examined. We will also test Hypotheses 5 and 6 and discuss the results.

ANALYSIS OF THREE DECISION MODES

The distribution of the three decision making modes among the four planning milieux is displayed in Table 12.1. It will be recalled from Chapter 5 that the three decision modes are "standardization," "negotiation," and "subjective."

Each strategy maker was required in Question 16 (see Appendix A) to indicate the perceived decision making mode of organizational members for five sub-areas of electronic banking. Thus each strategy maker had to provide a total of five responses concerning perceived decision modes, bringing the total number of responses by the 199 subjects involved to 995 (with 8 of the 207 subjects failing to respond to the relative item in the questionnaire). The top row relating to each planning milieu in the table gives the total number of times a particular decision mode has been indicated by the strategy makers in that planning milieu. For example, the "standardization" decision mode was indicated 112 times by the strategy makers who placed themselves in Planning Milieu I. The second row of each planning milieu gives the percentage of each decision mode among all the three possible modes. The third row indicates the percentages of each decision mode among all the planning milieux. Thus, 35.6

TABLE 12.1

Frequencies for Planning Milieux and Decision Modes

| Planning Milieu | Decision Mode Frequencies | | | |
	Standard ization	Nego tiation	Subjec tive	Total
I. Agreement is High for both Planning Objectives and Planning Horizon (N = 52)	112 43.1 35.6 11.3	120 46.2 25.2 12.1	28 10.8 13.8 2.8	260 26.1
II. Agreement is Low for Planning Objectives and High for Planning Horizon (N = 13)	11 16.9 3.5 1.1	36 55.4 7.5 3.6	18 27.7 8.9 1.8	65 6.5
III. Agreement is High for Planning Objectives and Low for Planning Horizon (N = 37)	74 40.0 23.5 7.4	75 40.5 15.7 7.5	36 19.5 17.7 3.6	185 18.6
IV. Agreement is Low for both Planning Objectives and Planning Horizon (N = 97)	118 24.3 37.5 11.9	246 50.7 51.6 24.7	121 24.9 59.6 12.2	485 48.7
Total (N=199)	315 31.7	477 47.9	203 20.4	995 100.0

Decision Mode frequencies are the totals of number of times respondents in a particular Planning Milieu have indicated a specific mode (the three modes making up a total of 5 for each respondent). The three lines of data for each Planning Milieu are the percentages for rows, columns, and total.

percent of all "standardization" mode frequencies was in Planning Milieu I, compared to only 3.5 percent in Planning Milieu II, and so on. The fourth and last row for each planning milieu shows the percentage of each decision mode within each planning milieu among the overall total frequency (995) of responses by all strategy makers (numbering 199).

A few points may be observed from the table. First, the number of times the "negotiation" mode has been indicated is more or less the same, around 50 percent, for all the four planning milieux (at 46.2, 55.4, 40.5, and 50.7 percent). Thus the other two decision modes in the aggregate account for half of the overall decision mode picture. The dominance of the negotiation mode in the strategic planning area is unexceptional, although its relatively high frequency is noteworthy. At least for this particular organization, WESTBANK, the strategy makers seem to be of the uniform opinion that for around half the time the strategic planning process attracts the negotiation mode, irrespective of the perceived degrees of agreement concerning planning objectives and planning horizons.

Second, on an overall basis, the decision mode most widely perceived next to "negotiation" (47.9 percent) was that of "standardization" (with 31.7 percent), followed by that termed "subjective" (20.4 percent). This indicates a perception of relatively standardized procedures existing in the strategic planning area. One implication of such a perception is that roughly one-third of the strategic decision making is thought of as determined by organizational routines and prescribed rules, leaving about one-fifth of the decision domain under the sway of subjective hunches, intuitions, and opinions. These percentages of perceived decision modes provide us with a fairly explicit picture of the way the strategy makers as a class perceive the decision making arena in the organization studied.

Third, the "standardization" mode in Planning Milieu I accounts for over 43 percent of the total frequency in that milieu, compared to only about 24 percent in the case of Planning Milieu IV. The opposite tendency is observed for the "subjective" mode, for which Planning Milieu I has about 11 percent while Planning Milieu IV has nearly 25 percent. Incidentally, these two opposing tendencies is an apparent artifact of the parameters of the question eliciting the decision mode counts. Each subject was restricted to exactly five responses, so that by placing more responses in one decision mode, say "standardization," he or she is necessarily deprived of the maximum potential opportunity of

TABLE 12.2

Frequencies and Percentages of Decision Modes

Number	Standard ization	Nego tiation	Subjec tive
0	84 (42.0)	42 (21.0)	107 (53.5)
1	34 (17.0)	37 (18.5)	35 (17.5)
2	27 (13.5)	34 (17.0)	35 (17.5)
3	17 (8.5)	22 (11.0)	5 (2.5)
4	14 (7.0)	14 (7.0)	7 (3.5)
5	24 (12.0)	51 (25.5)	11 (5.5)
Total	200 (100.0)	200 (100.0)	200 (100.0)

Numbers in parentheses represent percentages of the frequencies within each Decision Mode.

indicating the other two modes. However, since the subjects had complete choice for indicating all the three modes in any combination, the phenomenon of one dominating mode constraining the frequency of the other two is only apparently artifactual, and does not pose any problem in our analysis.

Fourth, directing our attention to the column headed "subjective," it will be observed that while Planning Milieu I had only 13.8 percent of the responses with 26.1 percent of the strategy makers, or a ratio of about half, each of the other three planning milieux had a ratio of more than 1. The indication clearly is that when any lack of agreement is perceived there is an increased perception of the "subjective" decision making mode. This is supportive of the line of reasoning outlined in Chapter 5.

The distribution of the frequencies of responses for the three decision modes is given in Table 12.2. The figures in the table represent the number of subjects indicating 0 to 5 responses for each decision mode, while the parentheses contain the percentages of subjects within each decision mode. Thus, 84 strategy makers (constituting 42.0 percent of the 200 subjects responding to the relative question) failed to indicate any "standardization" mode, while 34 strategy makers indicated one response for this mode, 27 indicated two responses, and so on.

An examination of the percentages reveal that slightly over half of the sample (53.5 percent) did not perceive the "subjective" mode at all in the strategic decision making of the organization. A similarly total absence of the "standardization" mode was perceived by 42 percent of the subjects (noted earlier for illustrative purposes), and of the "negotiation" mode by 21 percent. At the other extreme, 25.5 of the respondents perceived an unadulterated "negotiation" mode of decision making being adopted by organizational members at large. Interestingly, 5.5 percent of the strategy makers felt that a completely "subjective" mode of decision making prevailed in the organization. If the perceptions of the dominant decision mode among strategy makers is computed by summing up those indicating 3 or more responses in any one mode (leaving a minority of at most 2 responses for the other two modes), it transpires that 27.3 percent of the sample perceived the "standardization" mode, 43.5 percent the "negotiation" mode, and 11.5 percent the "subjective" mode. These percentages, in their aggregate, also serve to highlight the fact that as much as 82.3 percent of the strategy makers tended to clearly perceive a dominant mode of decision making.

TABLE 12.3

Standardization Mode and Organizational Level

Number	ESVP	VP	AVP	Total
0	14 (50.0)	43 (39.1)	27 (43.5)	84 (42.0)
1	2 (7.1)	25 (22.7)	7 (11.3)	34 (17.0)
2	4 (14.3)	19 (17.3)	4 (6.5)	27 (13.5)
3	3 (10.7)	10 (9.1)	4 (6.5)	17 (8.5)
4	2 (7.1)	6 (5.5)	6 (9.7)	14 (7.0)
5	3 (10.7)	7 (6.4)	14 (22.6)	24 (12.0)
Total	28 (100.0)	110 (100.0)	62 (100.0)	200 (100.0)
Mean	1.50	1.38	1.95	1.58
S.D.	1.82	1.52	2.10	1.77

Numbers in parentheses represent percentages of the frequencies within each Organizational Level.

TABLE 12.4

Negotiation Mode and Organizational Level

Number	ESVP	VP	AVP	Total
0	6 (21.4)	16 (14.5)	20 (32.3)	42 (21.0)
1	7 (25.0)	19 (17.3)	11 (17.7)	37 (18.5)
2	3 (10.7)	26 (23.6)	5 (8.1)	34 (17.0)
3	2 (7.1)	14 (12.7)	6 (9.7)	22 (11.0)
4	1 (3.6)	9 (8.2)	4 (6.5)	14 (7.0)
5	9 (32.1)	26 (23.6)	16 (25.8)	51 (25.5)
Total	28 (100.0)	110 (100.0)	62 (100.0)	200 (100.0)
Mean S.D.	2.43 2.04	2.54 1.75	2.18 2.05	2.41 1.89

Numbers in parentheses represent percentages of the
frequencies within each Organizational Level.

Frequencies of the decision mode perceptions at the three organizational levels are displayed in three separate tables, each table dealing with one mode. In Table 12.3, the "standardization" decision mode is analyzed. It will be observed that out of the 5 responses allowed each strategy maker, 1.58 responses were allocated to this mode on the average by strategy makers as a whole. However, while the AVPs had 1.95 responses assigned to this decision mode, the VPs had only 1.38 responses. The ESVPs, with a mean frequency of 1.50, were closest to the overall mean. Also, 50 percent of the ESVP group did not believe that this decision mode prevailed at all. Interestingly, over 22 percent of the AVP group believed that the character of decision making was clearly of the "standardization" mode only, a perception sharply in contrast with that of the ESVPs (10.7 percent) and VPs (6.4 percent).

An analysis similar to the preceding one is given in Table 12.4 in respect of the "negotiation" decision making mode. Here, the overall mean frequency is 2.41. While the VPs seem to allocate somewhat more (2.54) to this mode, the AVPs seem to perceive far less (2.18). Over 32 percent of the AVPs seem to eliminate any role for this mode, while nearly 26 percent believe this to be the only decision mode. For over 32 percent of the ESVPs this is the only mode, while over 21 percent do not see this at all.

The remaining analysis, for the "subjective" decision mode, is given in Table 12.5. The overall mean is 1.02 counts for this mode. The AVPs assigned a low 0.87 mean frequency, while both the other organizational levels somewhat higher frequencies at 1.07 and 1.08. Remarkably, fully 64.5 percent of the AVPs have seen no evidence of this mode at all among organizational members in general, while nearly 11 percent of the ESVPs consider that this is the only decision mode prevailing in the organization.

In an overall sense, though, there seems to be no significant difference between the three organizational levels in the perception of decision modes among organizational members. This is evident from Table 12.6. The implication clearly is that, given a specific organizational context, the perception of decision making modes adopted by members in general for strategic planning purposes is invariant across organizational levels. That being so, it could be expected that strategy makers in all levels would adopt more or less uniform approaches in regard to their own decision making modes for strategic planning activities.

TABLE 12.5

Subjective Mode and Organizational Level

Number	ESVP	VP	AVP	Total
0	15	52	40	107
	(53.6)	(47.3)	(64.5)	(53.5)
1	7	21	7	35
	(25.0)	(19.1)	(11.3)	(17.5)
2	2	26	7	35
	(7.1)	(23.6)	(11.3)	(17.5)
3	0	3	2	5
	(0.0)	(2.7)	(3.2)	(2.5)
4	1	3	3	7
	(3.6)	(2.7)	(4.8)	(3.5)
5	3	5	3	11
	(10.7)	(4.5)	(4.8)	(5.5)
Total	28	110	62	200
	(100.0)	(100.0)	(100.0)	(100.0)
Mean	1.07	1.08	0.87	1.02
S.D.	1.65	1.34	1.45	1.42

Numbers in parentheses represent percentages of the
frequencies within each Organizational Level.

TABLE 12.6

Decision Modes and Organizational Level

Decision Mode	ESVP (1)	VP (2)	AVP (3)	Significance Level of T-Tests		
				1:2	1:3	2:3
Standardization	1.500	1.382	1.952	n.s.	n.s.	.063
N	28	110	62			
Negotiation	2.429	2.536	2.177	n.s.	n.s.	n.s.
N	28	110	62			
Subjective	1.071	1.082	0.871	n.s.	n.s.	n.s.
N	28	110	62			

Significance levels were determined on the basis of
two-tailed t-tests using an estimate of separate variance.

RELATIONSHIP BETWEEN PLANNING MILIEUX
AND DECISION MODES

We now turn to the testing of the two remaining hypotheses of this study. Hypothesis 5 states that strategy makers in Planning Milieu I will perceive the use of "standardization" decision mode more than the strategy makers in Planning Milieu IV. In a somewhat complementary fashion, Hypothesis 6 states that strategy makers in Planning Milieu IV will perceive the use of "subjective" decision mode more than the strategy makers in Planning Milieu I. As evident from the analysis in Table 12.7, both the hypotheses were confirmed, the respective significance levels being $p < .003$ and $p < .001$.

The table also shows that there are no significant differences in the frequencies for the "negotiation" mode among the planning milieux (which are reduced to three types for analytical purposes, the two "mixed" ones in the middle, II and III, being combined). There is, however, a signifi-

TABLE 12.7

Planning Milieux and Decision Modes

Decision Mode	Planning Milieu			Significance Level of T-Tests		
	1	2+3	4	1:2+3	1:4	2+3:4
Standardization	2.154	1.700	1.217	n.s.	.003	.058
N	52	50	97			
Negotiation	2.308	2.220	2.536	n.s.	n.s.	n.s.
N	52	50	97			
Subjective	0.539	1.080	1.247	.028	.001	n.s.
N	52	50	97			

cantly higher incidence of the "subjective" mode in the "mixed agreement" planning milieux as compared to the "high agreement" Planning Milieu I. Looking at the relative frequencies of the "subjective" mode in the table, one notices the gradual progression in frequency from the "high agreement" Planning Milieu I, to the "mixed agreement" Planning Milieux II and III, and onto the "low agreement" Planning Milieu IV. A similar gradient in the frequencies is evident in the "standardization" mode, where the progression is in the reverse direction. Both these sets of frequencies are entirely in alignment with the theoretical framework developed in Chapter 5.

In regard to the "negotiation" decision mode -- which is partially a coalition building exercise --, the table does not show any particular pattern besides the uniformly high values already commented upon. However, it is a point of some interest that the highest frequency (2.536) occurs in Planning Milieu IV. It also turns out that this mode is the dominant one in that milieu. Taken together, these two facts allow us to infer that in a planning context perceived as one of relatively low agreement on planning objectives and planning horizons, the conditions seem most appropriate

TABLE 12.8

Standardization Mode in Planning Milieux I and IV

| | Standardization Mode in | | Significance |
	Plg Mil I	Plg Mil IV	Level of T-Tests
OVERALL	2.154	1.217	.003
N	52	97	
ORGANIZATIONAL LEVEL			
ESVP	1.375	1.000	n.s.
N	8	14	
VP	1.846	1.246	.075
N	26	57	
AVP	2.944	1.269	.008
N	18	26	

for a "negotiation" type of decision making in strategic planning.

Continuing with this line of reasoning, it is also observed from Table 12.7 that the most prevalent decision mode in the "high agreement" Planning Milieu I is, once again, one of "negotiation." This seems to indicate that strategy makers perceive substantial scope for "negotiation" when they also perceive substantial agreement prevailing about planning objectives and planning horizons. When the above comments are coupled with the fact that the "negotiation" mode has the lowest incidence (2.220) in the two "mixed agreement" planning milieux (II and III combined), it seems reasonable to suggest that the scope for "negotiation" decision mode is considered limited when the perceived situation is neither one of "high agreement" nor of "low agreement." Indeed, for the "mixed agreement" planning milieux, the "negotiation" mode is not a clearly dominant one vis-a-vis the other two modes.

TABLE 12.9

Subjective Mode in Planning Milieux I and IV

	Subjective Mode in		Significance
	Plg Mil I	Plg Mil IV	Level of T-Tests
OVERALL	0.539	1.247	.001
N	52	97	
ORGANIZATIONAL LEVEL			
ESVP	1.125	1.071	n.s.
N	8	14	
VP	0.423	1.404	.001
N	26	57	
AVP	0.444	1.000	.095
N	18	26	

In sum, the tentative explanation seems to be that when the perception is clear as to the nature of the planning context, either one of high or low consensus, the "negotiation" mode is believed to prevail. In other words, the conditions in such cases may be characterized as well clarified and delineated as regards the perceived consensus level (high or low) surrounding the object of negotiations. When, however, the perception of the strategy makers is one of relative confusion, with a "mixed" bag of agreement on one factor and disagreement on another, the conditions do not seem fit for the negotiation process to prosper. The explanation proposed above not only lends significance to the role of strategy maker perceptions -- a fundamental credo prompting this investigation --, but has obvious implications for the nature of the actions that are ineluctably predicated upon such perceptions.

In Table 12.8 the analysis for testing Hypothesis 5 is extended to the three organizational levels. While the directions of the "standardization" mode frequencies are as predicted for all the three groups, the differences between Planning Milieux I and IV are significant only for the AVPs (at p < .008). This may be indicative of the tendency for the higher level executives to perceive less of a role for standardized decision making procedures in strategic planning as compared to the lowest level AVPs. The conventional view of more discretionary content in the higher echelons of an organization would seem to be supported in this finding.

The detailed organizational level analysis relating to Hypothesis 6 is given in Table 12.9. Unlike in the preceding analysis, the desired direction is not evident for the ESVP group, albeit the discrepancy is not extraordinarily large. The other two groups show tendencies consistent with the hypothesis, although only one of them (VPs) shows a statistically significant difference (p < .001). The "subjective" decision mode is thus perceived in a somewhat less clear-cut manner by the strategy makers in Planning Milieux I and IV as compared to the "standardization" mode.

13
A REPLICATION
STUDY

In this chapter, summary comments will be made on the statistical analyses of the data collected from a second research site. This second banking organization, named EASTBANK here, provided an opportunity for replication of the main study carried out in WESTBANK. The analytical procedures employed are identical with the one that was adopted in the earlier chapters for the WESTBANK data. The discussion that follows will confine itself, in the main, with comparisons between the two samples. It may be useful to state at the outset that this replication has no extraordinary results to reveal. For the sake of convenience, all the statistical analysis tables relating to the EASTBANK replication sample have been placed in Appendix B, arranged in the same serial order as the tables for the main WESTBANK sample.

DESCRIPTIVE STATISTICS

The EASTBANK site was composed of two large departments of one of the world's largest international banking organizations, with headquarters in the eastern United States. The modalities of the investigation were agreed upon after extensive discussions with top executives of the bank's west coast offices. The questionnaire used was the same as that for WESTBANK, except that Question 3 concerning the functional areas of the respondents was different in its representative sub-categories.

A total of 173 subjects were employed in the two departments with corporate titles of VP and AVP. There was

only one EVP/SVP in these departments, and hence the decision had to be made to eliminate the ESVP organizational
level from the data gathering and analysis. This is one
important difference to bear in mind while making comparisons with the WESTBANK sample as a whole. A second difference is that only two selected departments were involved,
and not all of the corporate headquarters executives in the
potential population. All the subjects in the two departments were, however, included in the questionnaire survey.
The questionnaires were mailed to the respondents with a
cover letter from a senior executive of the bank, along with
a return envelope.

A total of 62 usable responses were received, so that
the overall response rate was 35.8 percent. Compared to the
other sample, this lower response rate could be partly
attributed to the remoteness of the research site and, perhaps of more consequence, the fact that no reminders were
sent.

The numbers of the questionnaires received are displayed in Table B.1 according to the different functional
areas and the two organizational levels. The functional
areas, it will be noticed from the table, differ from the
WESTBANK sample, in that they are in the nature of
Administration, Credit, Marketing, Operations, etc. The
earlier sample, it will be recalled, had the functional
areas as Branch Banking, International Banking, Corporate
Banking, and so on. It will be seen that there were 26 VPs
and 36 AVPs in the final sample of 62. The response rates
for the two organizational levels were much the same at 35.1
and 36.4 percent, as shown in Table B.2.

The intercorrelations among the variables are shown in
Table B.3. There are no significant differences with the
main sample in the overall pattern of correlations.

Some of the demographic statistics are displayed in
Table B.4, arranged according to the two organizational levels. There were 52 males and 10 females, which means that
the females (16.1 percent) were proportionately less than
that in the earlier sample (21.7 percent), and especially so
in the VP group (3.8 versus 15.8 percent).

The age distribution was not too different in the two
samples, although the second one tended to have a higher
representation in the bottom "upto 35 years" category at the
cost of the older "51 years and over" category. The mean
age of this sample was 38.5 years (compared with 42.5 years
in the main sample) with a standard deviation of 6.7 years.

The level of education shows some differences in terms
of a much higher percentage of graduate degree holders among

the AVPs (41.7 percent in this sample compared to only 12.9 percent in the first one).

In terms of the number of subjects at the two organizational levels, the difference is somewhat significant, in that it contained a higher number of AVPs (36) compared to VPs (26), whereas the main sample had many more VPs (114) than AVPs (62).

The job experience data are given in Table B.5. No extraordinary variations are noticeable as between the two samples.

RELATIONSHIP BETWEEN FUTURE TIME PERSPECTIVE
AND PLANNING HORIZONS

Tables B.6 through B.9 set out the various analyses relating to the future time perspective for the replication sample in the same manner as Tables 8.1 through 8.4 pertaining to the main sample. No general patterns of differences are evident.

The preferred planning horizon data and analyses are similarly laid out in Tables B.10 to B.12. The cut-off points for trichotomizing the FTP values were, however, slightly different in order to accommodate the different range and distribution of values (from 1.22 to 3.33, compared to the earlier sample's 1.33 to 3.11). These cut-off points were selected at 2.25 and 2.50 (rather than at 2.40 and 2.60 for the main sample). This resulted in 24 strategy makers being classified as belonging to the Near FTP group and 16 as belonging to the Distant FTP group. The cut-off points for the PLGHOR variable (range 0.50 year to 7.50 years; median 2.49 years) were, however, retained at 2 and 3 years respectively (see Table B.11).

Hypothesis 1 was confirmed at the $p < .001$ level of significance (see Chapter 6 for full statements of all hypotheses). Similar confirmations were also obtained at both the organizational levels. Table B.12 shows that the Short PLGHOR strategy makers had a significantly lower FTP compared to those with Long PLGHOR.

RELATIONSHIP BETWEEN FUTURE TIME PERSPECTIVE
AND PLANNING MILIEUX

Table B.13 gives the detailed organizational level data on the perceived degree of agreement about planning objectives.

The organizational level data on the perceived degree of agreement on planning horizons is shown in Table B.14.

Hypothesis 4 was confirmed at p < .004 significance level, as shown in Table B.15. At the individual organizational levels too the hypothesis was supported.

Data concerning the planning milieux are displayed in Table B.16. The percentage distribution of strategy makers among the four planning milieux was somewhat different from the main WESTBANK sample in regard to Planning Milieux I and IV, with the former milieu having a higher percentage (40.3 versus 32.3). In the earlier case, it was the other way round, with 26 percent in Planning Milieu I and 48 percent in Planning Milieu IV. This was probably due to the fact that the EASTBANK subjects, being part of a relatively homogeneous department, perceived a higher level of agreement among organizational actors than in the case of the WESTBANK's diverse corporate arena.

The statistics in Table B.17 failed to confirm Hypothesis 3 at a significant level, although the association was in the expected direction. An organizational level analysis showed that the reason for this failure lay in the VP group, in which the two means seemed to be related slightly in the opposite direction. The rather small numbers of the sub-sample could most likely have been responsisble for the skewed results.

Hypothesis 2 was confirmed at p < .002 level of significance (see Table B.18). At the VP level, however, the finding was not significant although the association was in the expected direction.

Table B.19 gives the results of the exploratory statistical analysis, confirming (at p < .003) that the strategy makers in Planning Milieux I and IV differed in their FTP score (as was also true of the larger sample).

RELATIONSHIP BETWEEN PLANNING MILIEUX
AND DECISION MODES

Frequency distributions of the three decision making modes are displayed in Tables B.20 through B.25. The overall percentages of the frequencies relating to the three decision modes as between themselves are similar in the two samples -- 31.7, 47.9, and 20.4 for the "standardization," "negotiation," and 'subjective" modes in the WESTBANK sample (see Table 12.1), compared to 27.1, 47.7, and 25.2 in the EASTBANK sample (Table B.20). However, the mean frequencies at the constituent organizatioal levels in the two samples

TABLE 13.1

Comparison of Decision Modes in Two Samples

Decision Mode	WESTBANK			EASTBANK		
	VP (N=110)	AVP (N=62)	Total (N=172)	VP (N=26)	AVP (N=36)	Total (N=62)
Standardization	1.38	1.95	1.58	1.58	1.19	1.36
Negotiation	2.54	2.18	2.41	2.04	2.64	2.39
Subjective	1.08	0.87	1.02	1.39	1.17	1.26

have different configurations. The relevant information is contained in Table 13.1, which has been constructed from the means data extracted from Tables 12.3 to 12.5 and B.22 to B.24.

It is clear that while the means for the "negotiation" mode are more or less the same (2.41 and 2.39), that for the "standardization" mode is lower in the EASTBANK sample (1.36 versus 1.58 of WESTBANK). In consequence, of course, the "subjective" mode is higher in the EASTBANK sample.

Examining the data at the organizational levels, sub-stantial differences are evident in the mean frequencies. In the EASTBANK sample, in comparison with the other one, the AVP group perceives less of the "standardization" mode (1.19 compared to 1.58), more of the "negotiation" mode

TABLE 13.2

Hypothesis Testing Results in Two Samples

	Significance Level	
Hypothesis	WESTBANK (N=207)	EASTBANK (N=62)
1	.001	.001
2	.001	.002
3	.002	n.s.
4	.001	.004
5	.003	.011
6	.001	n.s.

(2.64 versus 2.16), and more of the "subjective" mode (1.17 versus 0.87). In a similar fashion, the VP group in the EASTBANK sample differs with the main sample in terms of the following mean frequencies, noted in the above order: 1.58 versus 1.38, 2.04 versus 2.54, and 1.39 versus 1.08.

Overall, it appears that the VP group in EASTBANK perceives a lesser role for the "negotiation" mode and a more prominent one for the other two, in comparison with the corresponding subjects in WESTBANK. In contrast, the AVP group in EASTBANK perceives a more dominant role for the "negotiation" mode than their counterparts in WESTBANK, a less prominent role for the "standardization" mode, and a greater role for the "subjective" mode. In sum, the organizational level distribution of perceived decision making modes shows some differences as between the corporate-wide WESTBANK sample and the departmental EASTBANK sample.

The distributions of decision mode perceptions have no significant differences as between the two organizational levels (see Table B.25), as was also the case in the main sample.

The statistical findings relating to Hypotheses 5 and 6 are shown in Table B.26. Hypothesis 5 was confirmed at the p < .001 level of significance. However, Hypothesis 6 was not confirmed, although the association was in the expected direction.

Exploratory analyses of the organizational level differences relating to the two hypotheses are set out in Tables B.27 and B.28. The invalidation of Hypothesis 6 appears to be the result of the AVP group having a slightly higher (rather than lower, as hypothesized) mean frequency of the "subjective" mode in Planning Milieu I compared to Planning MIlieu IV.

COMPARATIVE FINDINGS OF MAIN STUDY
AND REPLICATION

A summary display of the results of testing all the hypotheses in the two samples is given in Table 13.2. Certain other exploratory analyses, notably concerning the organizational levels, have also elicited substantive findings, but are not shown in the table. It will be observed that except for two cases, Hypotheses 2 and 6 for the replication EASTBANK sample only, all the hypotheses of this study were confirmed.

PART IV
IMPLICATIONS FOR RESEARCH AND PRACTICE

14
IMPLICATIONS FOR
STRATEGY MAKING RESEARCH

The results of this study have been discussed at some length in the previous chapters. Some further observations, however, remain to be made regarding the implications of those findings for two broad areas of endeavor. The first concerns the implications for further research, which we will discuss in this chapter. The second area relates to the implications for management practice in general and the strategy making enterprise in particular, and will be covered in the next chapter. Discussions on both these areas will include remarks of a recommendatory nature as an impetus for implementing the logical next steps which seem to be suggested by this investigation.

In addition to the two substantive areas noted above, we will also offer some remarks of a general nature concerning certain facets of the subject matter of this study. These concluding remarks, while not associated with the study hypotheses in a direct manner, are nevertheless considered significant to the gestalt informing the thinking and motivation behind this research. They should serve, it is hoped, to imbed this investigation in the larger program of trying to understand the nature and role of strategy makers qua individual actors.

DEVELOPING MORE DISTANT FUTURE ORIENTATION

In terms of the data on individual future time perspective of strategy makers in this study, a majority of the 177 respondents in the WESTBANK sample were concentrated at the lower end of the FTP scale (the mean was 2.411 in a possible range of between 1 and 4, with a median of 2.435, a standard deviation of 0.358, and a range of 1.778). As much as 57.6 percent had scored below 2.5, the midpoint of the scale.

In view of the significance of future orientation, it would be worthwhile to consider whether ways could be found to increase the FTP scores of strategy makers. Stated otherwise, the problem is one of increasing the FTP score of strategy makers from the current mean of 2.411 (which is closer to the "near" future subzone than the "distant" subzone) to somewhere beyond the midpoint of the scale. This question of course assumes that it is a desirable objective in particular organizational circumstances to foster more distant future time perspectives (May, 1982; Paskins, 1985). The case for imparting knowledge on the subject of the future in our schools has been on the educational policy agenda for some time (Toffler, 1974).

Research is obviously needed to learn more about this significant question. There is currently hardly any research published on the subject. However, there are certain tentative indications that the possibility of extending an individual's future orientation may not be ruled out altogether. One example of how this could be accomplished is available from the research reported by El Sawy (1983). The subjects were asked by the researcher to deliberate upon the distant past in terms of the history of the organization in which they worked. Later, they were directed to think about the future. It was found that the participants visualized longer planning time horizons in their images of the future. It would thus appear that an initial consideration of the distant organizational past facilitates the follow-up development of more elongated planning horizons.

Clearly, the concept of the future in strategic planning needs to be grasped on the basis of an actual ability to do so. It is, of course, critical that sufficient care is exercised to avoid being seduced into mundane extrapolations that would in fact occur in the absence of that distinctive ability. Some strategy makers, as has been found in this study, have a more distant future time perspective than others. Any lengthening of that perspective has to be in substantive terms -- a change which one would expect to be reflected in an actual increase in the FTP score with the instrument used here. An elongation of the planning time horizon may not necessarily imply an additional gain in future time perspective in real terms. As we noted earlier, only a substantive grasp of the future validates a distant future time perspective. Longer planning horizons determined without the supporting individual distant future orientation may not be anything more than the fruit of simple extrapolations.

We may note here that the major proposals in the literature about fostering long-term orientation among corporate executives have restricted themselves to various forms of incentives built into the compensation structure (Stonich, 1984). The hope is that the executives would somehow curb their eagerness to look good in the quarterly performance race in order to win ultimately in a longer time frame with all its uncertainties. This kind of incentive mechanism has not worked so far in U.S. industry, for reasons too well known to warrant repetition here. Some other methods of achieving a longer future orientation among our executives deserve to be considered (Adelson, 1985). As an example, it appears that having more inside directors on company boards could lead to longer range thinking and better performance, as research in Japanese enterprises indicates (Fujimori, 1983). Interestingly, the Japanese managers seem to generally have longer planning horizons than their American and British counterparts (Keys and Miller, 1984; Kono, 1984).

INSTRUMENTATION FOR MEASURING INDIVIDUAL FUTURE TIME PERSPECTIVE

The need for a more reliable instrument for assessing the future time perspective of organizational members is clearly imperative. The insights gained in this study could be more fully applied in the corporate sphere if a measuring instrument is developed which is appropriate for widespread practical use. The particular requirements of administering the instrument to corporate executives and other business people should of course be kept in mind.

The research instrument at present is based on the listing of important events in one's personal future. Its use is dependent on the respondent being unaware of the precise purpose of the exercise. In a corporate situation, in which suspicion and cynicism about research instruments cannot be ruled out, it is imperative that a much more reliable approach be developed.

There is some evidence of efforts to refine the procedures in the general area of temporal orientations, such as the self-administered paper-and-pencil test on psychological predispositions toward time developed by Settle, Alreck, and Belch (1981). Much more work, however, is plainly needed on the subject of temporal perspective, but especially for improving the method of assessing individual future time perspective. This work would seem to lie within the province of the psychologists, but some interest and intellectual prodding by the strategic management research establishment should be in order.

The particular technique used in this investigation is an adaptation of the instrument used by Cottle (1968, 1976). It was adequate for the exploratory purposes of this study. However, the instrument would need to be developed further to assure increased methodological rigor, in terms particularly of its reliability and validity. The results of the study are sufficiently interesting to warrant developing the instrument further for profitable future research purposes.

Furthermore, the instrument used in this study was adequate for a one-time administration. However, if longitudinal studies are contemplated, as would be necessary for further studies regarding the changes in temporal perspective over the lifetime of a respondent, more sophisticated instrumentation would be required. Toward that end, it would be of advantage, in terms of increased reliability and validity, to administer the improved instrument to executives in different corporate settings and industries. The part played by situational factors in confounding the results of the subjectively-based instrument could also be studied with these data from diverse replications. In the process, additional insights into the nature of individual future time perspective may also be forthcoming.

RESEARCHER VALUES ABOUT THE FUTURE

As a general point, it needs to be acknowledged that any piece of research is much influenced by personal, social, and philosophical values associated with the researcher. The very interest in the future, the importance accorded to the future time perspective of individual strategy makers, and the significance assigned to the future dimension in the process of strategy making, are all indicative of certain values held implicitly by this author. The discerning reader surely needs no cautioning that others may not share, or so diligently subscribe to, the view that the subjective orientations of individual strategy makers have central significance. Or that the perspective on the future and the perception of planning milieux should count for as much as they appear to do in this investigation.

These remarks may seem to be somewhat superfluous, in that the value orientations of the researcher are generally recognized to have their due place in the evaluation of a research investigation. As Perrow (1980:261) observes astutely: "We all bring different intentions to the study of organizations; we are all like small children in a sandpit, playing at different fantasies, only occasionally acknowledging the other children." A few observations would seem to be in order on at least two counts. First, although the temporal dimension is an inseparable feature of the strategy making enterprise, its very all-pervasiveness has paradoxically resulted in its unthinking neglect in the research community. Second, the very construct of time has historically attracted a confusing array of definitions.

The variegated nature of this construct is evident from the different values that people attach to the notion of the future time dimension. To quote Bennis (1970:431) on this point:

> For me the "future" is a portmanteau word. It embraces several notions. It is an exercise of the imagination which allows us to compete with and try to outwit future events. Controlling the anticipated future is, in addition, a social invention that legitimizes the process of forward-planning. ... Most importantly, the future is a conscious dream, a set of imaginative hypotheses groping toward whatever vivid utopias lie at the heart of our consciousness.

While this is not the forum for expatiating upon the conceptual complexities of the time construct, suffice it to note that the idea of the future itself is a many-splendored phenomenon. This is because psychologically the future "embraces several notions." Hence, when a strategy maker attempts to fashion corporate decisions on the basis of a perception of that multi-faceted phenomenon called "the future," a plethora of interpretations is bound to emerge (Das, 1984). This multiplicity of interpretations and appreciations of the future time dimension is perhaps a result of the fact that the human agency (the strategy maker), while existing in the present time, is attempting to perceptually grasp, in the same present time, an unknown commodity like the future.

The proliferation of interpretations is very likely in the event of such conjunctions of somewhat contradictory characteristics of the two entities -- the human agent and the future as perceived by that agent. The first one, the human agent, is everlastingly rooted in the present even while attempting to perceive the "unknowable" conditions constituting the future. And the second entity -- the inexorably advancing future -- remains inscrutably aloof and unrevealing despite all perceptual entreaties.

Despite its intractable character, the future time dimension deserves to be studied because the strategy making enterprise is not only housed in the temporal dimension, but is also a fundamental element of that enterprise. The temporal dimension, thus, at once gives life to the strategy making enterprise and is a part of it.

FROM CONTEXT TO CONTENT OF THE STRATEGY MAKING PROCESS

As matters stand today, the temporal dimension is incorporated into the strategic planning process only at the most pedestrian level of clock or calendar time. It is critical that strategy makers become aware of the very real and prevalent tendency to base the thinking about planning mostly on past experiences and hindsight. It is pertinent to refer to the old saw about generals unwittingly preparing for the next war by being smarter at ensuring a victory in the last one. Strategy makers need to raise their consciousness about the cognitive trap of relying too faithfully on the reinterpreted lessons of the past to plot the course of the future.

> History in hand, people who select interpretations for present enactments usually see in the present what they have seen before. In the strategy formulation process in organizations, hindsight is a primary determinant of current planning. Outcomes from previous decisions, especially the mistakes, are disproportionately salient in current thinking. Musings such as "We should have gone into home computers 5 years ago," and "Digital watches were a loser," have greater bearing on current interpretations than the current events being interpreted. (Weick and Daft, 1983:75-76)

The discussion here has been motivated by the conviction that the subjective appreciation of the passage of time, especially future time, by the individual strategy makers is a relevant aspect of the strategic process. There is very little discussion at present about this temporal dimension in the business field. The process of strategy making being intimately concerned with the future time dimension, it stands to reason that the need is all the more critical for a richer understanding of the relationship between the future time perspectives of individual strategic actors and different facets of the planning process.

Research on the role of the future time perspective in strategy making needs to move from the current condition of "ignorance is bliss" to one of "knowing that you don't know." Davis (1982:65) has called this a shift in the "context" through a process of "transformation." He refers to the subsequent shift to a state of "knowing" as one of "change," providing what he calls "content." To borrow his terminology, the aim of this investigation has been to attempt a "transformation of the context" of research concerning the strategy making process by demonstrating that the time perspective of the individual strategy maker deserves serious examination. One needs to know that not much is known at present about the part that the future time perspective plays in the strategy making process. Only by going some way toward understanding the relevance of this altered or transformed context will it become feasible to effectively address questions about appropriate "changes in the content" of strategic planning.

One of the obvious ways to make a start at transforming the context of researching the strategy making process in terms of the subjective side of strategy making is to study the phenomenon of individual future time perspective in different kinds of organizations and in different industries (as also, of course, in different cultures). The research reported here should serve to provide the initial substantive justification to undertake such a transformation of the research context, in anticipation of further inquiry concerning content questions on the strategy making process.

The generalizability of the findings of this study would clearly depend on further supportive results from future replications of the kind mentioned above. The value of this future research would of course be enhanced considerably with more sophisticated techniques of measuring individual future time perspectives (discussed earlier).

In due course, it should also be worthwhile to extend the inquiry into the area of relationships between individual future time perspective and other variables, such as ideology, values, ethics, locus of control, expected tenure in an organization, relative importance of specific types of information for performing one's job, level of perceived environmental turbulence, and so on.

Once the context of strategy making is transformed adequately to accommodate the subjective temporal dimension of strategy makers -- with perhaps some more investigations along the lines of the present one --, it should not prove too onerous to launch some of the suggested follow-up explorations.

A WIDER RESEARCH PERSPECTIVE

The motivation for this research was provided by the general conviction that the extant emphasis on the rational-analytic mode in strategy making needs to be complemented (and not supplanted) with an examination of the subjective side (perceptions, values, ideologies, temporal perspectives, etc.) of the strategy maker qua a center-stage corporate actor. It was felt that such an understanding of the interaction between the rational and the subjective would help explain, for instance, why different top executives adopt different approaches to strategy making. This understanding should be useful in developing a well-balanced theoretical framework of the strategy making process.

A reasonable starting phase of a research program, in conformance with the thinking above, would be to study CEOs and other executives. This would help in better appreciating the manner in which the individual subjective attributes of the CEOs, such as perceptual and temporal orientations, "condition" the character of strategy making via action regarding data selection, analytic schema employed, judgment processes, and strategy selection, implementation, and evaluation.

Research is also needed to ascertain the part played by demographic and other background characteristics of top executives in the shaping of organizational performance. This should also go some way toward helping develop more effective policies for the utilization of the valuable human resource that a strategy maker is. After all, the most critical element of strategic human resource management is the management of the most critical human resource, namely, the strategy maker.

Methodologiclly, this question could be addressed initially through the use of large scale semi-structured interviews and surveys. This would permit content and cluster analysis as the analytic tools to start with. Eventually, a more sophisticated language than exists now should evolve to articulate the dynamics of the human agency in the strategic enterprise.

This research program should help in developing insights into the nature of the impact that the subjective constitution of strategy makers has in the making of strategy. The enticing proposition to explore, in other words, has to do with the extent to which the "nature" of the strategy maker is responsible for the character of a corporate strategy. Such knowledge would have significant implications for different executive suitabilities for diverse aspects of strategy making.

The study reported here was designed as a preliminary part of that program, concerning itself as it did with studying the relationships between the temporal perspectives of top executives, their perceptions of the planning context, their preferences for particular planning horizons, and their perceptions of decision modes adopted by organizational members in the area of strategic planning. Clearly, further studies need to be undertaken to follow through with the program, covering different aspects of strategy making. It is hoped that the present effort would be of some help toward that end.

15
IMPLICATIONS FOR THE
PRACTICE OF STRATEGY MAKING

The remarks in this chapter, while categorized for expository purposes as managerial practice, should be considered in tandem with those in the preceding chapter on research implications. In the field of strategy making, it would be difficult to compartmentalize the practice and research aspects if one were seeking to understand the reality of the strategy making enterprise.

SUBJECTIVITY IN THE STRATEGY MAKING PROCESS

The practicing managers may find that the subjective framework of the strategy making process presented in Chapter 2 helps them to deal more effectively with the environmental conditions. They should find it of advantage in visualizing the closed-loop nature of the process, wherein the environmental consequences of implementing their planned strategies are presented to them once again through their own perceptions of the environment (Schulman, 1976). The emphasis of the process framework on the perceptual element should also result in learning to understand why and how certain approaches to strategy making do not in fact result in anticipated outcomes. The notion of learning while engaged in the strategy making process is of some importance to practitioners, and deserves the attention of researchers. Organizations have been found to manage and revise the strategy making process to cope with the perceived changes and challenges in the environment (Miller and Friesen, 1983; Nottenburg and Fedor, 1983; Nystrom and Starbuck, 1984). As it often happens, the assumptions of planned strategies may

be found to be incorrect or irrelevant, and this can be seen
readily to be in the very first stage of the process model.
The observations of Eden, Jones, Sims, and Smithin (1981:38)
relating to the manner in which people in organizations handle complex, ill-structured policy issues seem particularly
relevant:

> Our experience as well as our conceptual orienta-
> tion leads us to believe that the "policy" issues
> perceived by individuals are inevitably character-
> ized by important idiosyncratic beliefs and val-
> ues, and concerns about the internal politics of
> the organization and relationships with other team
> members some, if not all, of which are likely to
> be crucial to policy choices perceived and made.

The model proposed here should be helpful to organizations
in accounting for the substantive role of perceptions of the
planning environment by individual strategic actors, rather
than relying, as currently, on purely "objective" information and the assumption of a completely rational decision
making mode in strategy making.

In a recent study of general managers, Kotter
(1982a:140-141) found that many organizations "impose a
rigid 'number crunching' requirement on the GM which often
does not require much strategic thinking in agenda setting."
In the area of technological development, Hayes and
Abernathy (1980:70) have decried the inordinate reliance on
analytical techniques on the part of American managers:

> Responsibility for this competitive listlessness
> belongs not just to a set of external conditions
> but also to the attitudes, preoccupations, and
> practices of American managers. ... during the
> past two decades, American managers have increas-
> ingly relied upon principles which prize analyt-
> ical detachment and methodological elegance over
> insight, based on experience, into the subtleties
> and complexities of strategic decisions.

Gradually, though, it is becoming plain that such an
inordinate stress on the rational-analytic dimension of
managerial practices needs to be tempered by a recognition
of the ineluctable role of subjective factors (Eden, Jones,
and Sims, 1979; Hurst, 1984; Kets de Vries and Miller, 1984;
Mintzberg and Waters, 1983; Mitroff, 1983; Mitroff and
Mason, 1983; Peters and Waterman, 1982; Ohmae, 1982; Pondy,

1984). For instance, Ronchi (1980) concludes that "extra-rational or even irrational elements intervene in the process of strategic adaptation, caused primarily by complexity and by the social-heuristic nature of planning" (p. 661), and observes that it is "essential to maximize in the organization the synergic effect of rational and extra-rational contributions" (pp. 667-668). A vigorous consideration of the role of subjective perceptions of strategy makers, as argued here, should serve to bring a sense of balance to the study of managerial practice in the area of strategy making (in management education as well as in research).

SIGNIFICANCE OF INDIVIDUAL FUTURE ORIENTATION

There is no research reported in the literature about the relevance of the individual future time perspective in the strategy making enterprise. The utility of conceiving and measuring the individual FTP of strategy makers has been demonstrated in this investigation with respect to the determination of an appropriate corporate planning horizon. It was found that there is a significant contingent association between near and distant future orientations of strategy makers on the one hand and short and long planning horizons of the organization on the other. It is as if there is an isomorphism between the psychological temporal environment of a strategy maker and the organizational planning horizon, much as would be expected from the ecological "law of requisite variety" (Ashby, 1968).

Thus, only the strategy makers with distant future orientation would be equipped to engage realistically in longer-period planning decisions. The clear implication is that only such strategy makers as have an adequate appreciation of time-passage in the long-term future could be expected to attend to long range planning. Strategy makers who have near future orientations would, by the same logic, be ill-suited to perform activities which have a long temporal reach. In the event that such long range planning tasks were allocated to them, these near future type of strategy makers would, as we have argued, be effectively extrapolating essentially a near-term appreciation or grasp of the future time zone. Note, for instance, the following typical observation based on field research in a corporate division:

> While all business plans provide estimates of a variety of quantitative measures for five years, often they are no more than mechanical extrapola-

tions of a more or less arbitrarily assumed growth rate. In fact, it is rare for serious effort to be invested in the longer range forecasts in the plan, even though ... the planning cycle for a new facility is often two years or more." (Bower, 1970:46-47)

The phenomenon of unthinking extrapolation in corporations, such as the one cited above, is sometimes recognized by researchers. However, it is rarely treated other than in a peripheral sense in the corporate planning literature. Some refreshingly candid observations, though, are available in Tregoe and Zimmerman (1980). Based on their experience of strategy formulation by senior executives in over two hundred major organizations all over the world spread over a decade, they make the following points about the essentially extrapolatory and short-range nature of the actual practice of long range planning:

Long-range plans tend to be based on projections of current operations into the future. ...

The extrapolation from the present mentioned above occurs despite many of the writings in the field which urge the establishment of objectives up-front as part of long-range planning. ... They are forced to build their future on the foundation of the projections rather than on a clear definition of what they want their organization to be. ...

Long-range plans are built up from the lowest levels, where information exists to make projections. ... The comment of one chief executive immersed in the planning cycle is typical: "By the time we get through with our long-range planning cycle, we are all so engrossed in the precision of our projections that we have lost our ability to question whether they are taking us where we want to go."

Long-range plans invariably tend to be overly optimistic. This results primarily from the desire of those making the projections at various levels of the organization to do better in their respective areas in the years ahead. ...

Long-range planning is really more short-range than anyone cares to admit. Long-range planning theory suggests that planning should project out five years and then recede back to the first year. But how can this be done in the absence of a structured framework for looking ahead five years? Lacking this, the sheer force of necessity leads managers to reverse the theory and begin by projecting from the first year. (Tregoe and Zimmerman, 1980:23-27)

The occurrence of the kind of straightforward extrapolations described above are evidently quite widespread. Unfortunately, it is difficult to determine the fact of these extrapolations in a rigorous manner. Strategy makers confidently draw up scenarios of the future, without any thought about the possibility that this may be no more than some casual conjectures rather than the fruit of special judgments and insights about the future (Das, 1983). The possibility of long-term planning being merely simple projections of the present is not widely recognized. The danger of an unquestioned acceptance of such mundane projections as valued judgments is apparent. Efforts need to be made to learn more about how strategy makers go about constructing such subjective projections, based on their tacit knowledge of the future. Meanwhile, the organizational implication clearly is that certain strategy makers are more suited than others for particular planning periods, long or short.

FUTURE PERFECT THINKING

The conception of the future time perspective can be further elaborated in terms of the future-perfect tense. Since planning has to do with actions, the manner in which a strategy maker projects actions in the future needs to be understood. According to Schutz (1967), a person contemplating an action in the future would think about it as if the action had already taken place. Planned action could, in that sense, be considered as occurring in the future perfect tense. As Schutz (1967:61) explains:

the actor projects his action as if it were already done with and lying in the past. It is a full-blown, actualized event, which the actor pictures and assigns to its place in the order of experiences given to him at the moment of projection. Strangely enough, therefore, because it is

pictured as completed, <u>the planned act bears the</u>
<u>temporal character of pastness</u>. ... The fact that
it is thus pictured as if it were simultaneously
past and future can be taken care of by saying
that it is thought of in the future perfect tense.

The dynamics of anticipating future events in the manner explicated above have clear relevance for strategy makers in a business organization. Engaged as they are in
taking actions in accordance with some plan lying in the
future time dimension, the ability to think in the future
perfect tense takes on particular significance. And the
farther a strategy maker is able to project such future perfect thinking, the greater is the possibility of realizing
planned actions. A related notion that is well recognized
is the vision of leaders (Bennis and Nanus, 1985).

The interesting point is that different strategy makers
have different perspectives of the future. Precisely
because strategy makers would need to anticipate events (in
the future perfect way), and thereby influence the choice of
appropriate actions, the depth of that anticipation would be
a material factor. As has been argued here, the more elongated the perspective an individual has of the future time
dimension, the more likely it is that the individual would
be planning for actions over a longer time period on the
basis of that perspective rather than on mundane and
"unknowing" extrapolation.

APPROPRIATE PLANNING HORIZONS

The strategy makers in the study felt that three years
was the appropriate planning horizon for their bank in the
area of electronic banking. The specific figures were a
mean of 2.85 years and a median of 2.76 years for the
WESTBANK sample. The bank's formal strategic planning horizon was five years. Thus, the mean of 2.85 years preferred
by the strategy makers was significantly lower than the
official norm followed in the actual strategic planning process. The five-year horizon is also most widely reflected
both in the academic literature and in practice.

The group of distant future oriented strategy makers in
this investigation believed that three years was the appropriate planning horizon. The near future oriented strategy
makers preferred an even shorter period. These data, it
should be remembered, reflect the best judgment of the
strategy makers. It seems reasonable to infer that, given

their individual judgment and future orientation, any significantly different planning period (such as five years)
would be only a superficial paper figure. The decisions and
actions of the strategy makers would have little relevance,
in real terms, to the formally set planning horizon. This
lends credence to the observation of Tregoe and Zimmerman
(1980:27) quoted earlier, namely, that "long-range planning
is really more short-range than anyone cares to admit."

We are not, however, concerned with the absolute figures of preferred planning horizons in this investigation.
The most appropriate planning cycle would be contingent on
the specific planning context. The precise planning horizon, thus, would largely be determined "existentially" or on
a normative basis.

Our interest lies in the implications of these preferences for actual practice. Planning horizon preferences
which are more near-term than the bank's formal planning
period would seem to indicate that the executives are com-
pelled to compromise their best judgment. In other words,
the arbitrarily imposed official five-year strategic planning period does not imply that the executives concerned are
in practice looking that long into the future. Most of them
could well be merely extrapolating their individual near-
term insights based primarily on a near future time perspective.

An identical argument holds true for organizations
which may have, for example, a fixed one-year or two-year
planning cycle, determined without regard to the distant
future oriented people participating in the strategic planning process. In this case, there is a contrary compulsion
for the executives to reign in their distant future orientation, so as to be able to participate within the restrictive
temporal ambit.

EXECUTIVE SUITABILITIES

Given the finding of differential future orientations
of strategy makers, it would be worth considering whether it
would be desirable to assign executives to different aspects
of the strategy making process based these orientations.
This approach of selective allocation of tasks and responsibilities may not always be feasible in a particular organization or at a particular point in time. Nor are there
clear guidelines as to how to identify such placement candi-
dates. Nevertheless, if the attribute of future orientation
were kept in mind, some managerial discretion could be exer-

cised in assessing executive suitabilities for different responsibilities. The literature indicates certain analogous notions for managerial assignments based on types of strategy, product life cycles, business conditions, and so forth (Gerstein and Reisman, 1983; Kerr, 1982; Leontiades, 1982; Wissema, van der Pol, and Messer, 1980). A point to note is that the need for any drastic changes in the existing planning periods would be minimized if such executive redeployments are carried out. This refers to the earlier discussion about the disadvantages of having a formal planning period which is inappropriate to the temporal orientations of executives.

Evidently, therefore, the placement of executives in accordance with their future orientations would help in better utilization of their capabilities. It would also help reduce their unease in having to function within a mismatched temporal frame. If distant future oriented executives, for instance, were required to engage in short-term activities, it would be reasonable to presume that they would be dissatisfied about the procrustean planning cycle. The opposite would be the case with near future oriented executives in a long-term task situation. Reflecting on the nature of current management practices, it seems both job competence and job satisfaction are being jeopardized in the laissez faire allocation of strategy making responsibilities that typically obtains in most business organizations.

Obviously, further research is needed on the subject, especially to learn about about how well the suggestions made above lead to more effectiveness in the strategy making process. It is not as if the strategy makers have not used their future thinking capabilities. Rather, it is now necessary to develop, in a systematic manner, an agenda for the conscious utilization of future orientations as a factor in the management of the strategy making process.

DIFFERENTIAL PERCEPTIONS OF PLANNING MILIEUX

The role of goal-means trade-offs in decision making was discussed in Chapter 5 in terms of planning objectives and planning horizons. The point was made that the perceptions of strategy makers about the internal planning context, or organizational milieu, would be expected to differ according as they had "near" or "distant" future time perspective. Specifically, it was reasoned that strategy makers with near future time perspective would be more likely to perceive a higher degree of consensus among organizational members with regard to both planning objectives and planning horizons. The hypotheses dealing with this point were confirmed.

The implications of this finding for managerial practice are in two major areas. First, if strategy makers do indeed perceive the planning milieu of the organization in the contingent manner implicit in the findings, then it challenges the traditional conception of an undifferentiated planning environment for all organizational members. It provides grounds for reassessing the management's unexamined assumptions about the planning environment. Thus far, the assumption has been that the internal planning environment is more or less the same for all strategy makers. The research reported here shows empirically that this may not be true. Indeed, the variations in perceived planning milieux are quite substantial among strategy makers. Different strategy makers tend to see the character of the planning milieux in distinctly different ways, both in terms of the perceptions of relative consensus and the three modes of decision making adopted by organizational members.

The second implication has to do with the finding that these different perceptions are contingently related to the future time perspectives of the strategic actors. This insight affords corporate managements with some leverage in terms of grasping the nature of the differential perceptions of organizational members. Once managements are aware of the existence of such perceptual differences regarding planning milieux, associated with individual future time perspectives, they can begin to incorporate that insight into various policy prescriptions. The implications will be in terms of possible changes in the planning environment (including the three principal strategic decision modes that were considered) through a reassignment of strategy makers of different categories (based on future time perspective).

But furthermore, in a simple and immediate way, the mere awareness of the phenomenon may lead to a more comprehensive approach to the assignment of strategy makers for different aspects of the strategic planning process and different kinds of planning. This is in line with the existing analogous case of factoring in such attributes as risk-taking propensity, ideologies, values, etc. The question of differential executive suitabilities, discussed earlier, for various aspects of the planning process is thus a question that managements would need to address.

It is no doubt true that factors such as risk-propensity or ideologies are difficult for the researcher to assimilate into the decision making rubric. What is being urged here is not that the future time perspective is an easy or tangible bit of information about subjective attributes. Rather, just as in the case of risk-taking behavior, the awareness of the factor serves to alert the relevant decision making authority to take it into account. For example, the ramifications of the individual future time perspective may be weighed in making decisions about strategy maker assignments. The individual future time perspective is, in that sense, yet another factor which plays a role in the determination of the character of the internal organizational context of planning or planning milieu. In sum, the findings reported here provide organizations with an additional factor to take into account in understanding and designing the internal organizational environment for the strategic planning enterprise.

CONSENSUS ON PLANNING OBJECTIVES AND PLANNING HORIZONS

The perception of consensus on planning objectives and planning horizons is critical for the successful implementation of any corporate plan. The attainment of coordinated effort being the rationale for plan implementation, it is necessary for each individual to be reassured that all other organizational members are conversant with (if not indeed also supportive of) the planning objectives and planning horizons. The perception of shared knowledge of objectives, and the resulting conviction that everybody is aware of what direction the organization intends to go, is the minimum condition for exerting oneself. Without this perceived consensus, no member is likely to be duly enthused about working purposefully.

The lack of perceived consensus strikes at the very heart of motivation to work. To even begin to meaningfully exert effort in an organizational situation, it is necessary that the individual perceives that all members are at least in agreement about what precisely are the planning objectives and planning horizons of the organization.

We have examined the phenomenon of perceived consensus, as delineated above, with data obtained from a large sample of senior executives (see Chapter 10). The results, as hypothesized, indicated that the degree of consensus could best be characterized as only moderate, considerably less than substantial, and certainly far less than complete. Also, as between the two areas of planning objectives and planning horizons, it was found that the perceived consensus about planning horizons was significantly less than about planning objectives.

This would seem to confirm the notion that the temporal dimension of planning is paid less attention in the corporate planning process in comparison with the dissemination of planning objectives. The fact that the planning horizon is a means to attaining planning objectives is somehow not consciously acknowledged. This is a serious deficiency, for the means constitute in many ways the more problematic component of a plan. More attention is thus called for in the area of the means-like temporal dimension (discussed in the next section).

The implications of the results are in two areas. First, organizations need to pay more attention to the hitherto neglected area of planning periods or horizons, so that all organizational members are aware of it as much as they are about planning objectives. The reason is that, as discussed below, the planning period is in reality, though at an implicit level, a potent area for what can be termed as the "silent politics of time." People negotiate and adapt objectives by "trading-off" on the temporal dimension.

Secondly, it is not enough to pay exclusive attention to the content of planning objectives. Organizations need to find ways to cultivate a perception among its members that there is a high degree of at-large consensus about planning objectives and planning horizons. It is easy to see the confusion that may be created if individual managers fail to perceive a general consensus among the entire body of organizational members about these matters. Given such a perceived lack of consensus, it would be very difficult to motivate organizational members along any strategic direction. A realistic evaluation of their performance would be equally problematic. One cannot blame a person for not being motivated to perform some activity if the person perceives substantial confusion about the nature of that activity persisting among organizational members. Similarly, without a perception of consensus on the time frame, the evaluation of performance also becomes seriously flawed.

The results reported here, while restricted in its ready generalizability by its selective sample, nevertheless afford sufficient grounds to warrant serious investigation into the phenomenon of less-than-adequate consensus levels obtaining in the uppermost echelons of corporations about planning objectives and planning horizons.

PLANNING HORIZON AS A MEANS

The organizational planning horizon can be visualized as the "means" component in the conventional goal-means matrix. Decision making in organizations is conditional on the balancing of goals and means (Simon, 1976; Lindblom, 1959). Taylor and Hawkins (1972:62) have explained this point as follows:

> Goals, like resources, have time-based utility. A new product developed, a plan put on stream, a degree of market penetration, become significant strategic objectives only if accomplished by a certain time. Delay may deprive them of all strategic significance.

It may be useful here to draw an analogy between time and money as different forms of virtual meta-resources. Just as money, which can be converted into various forms of resources or means, the time horizon can be treated as a virtual meta-resource in the planning context, enabling an organization to effectively convert it into, or trade it off against, other forms of resources or means.

One of the ways of examining the notion of planning horizon as a means is to discuss briefly the metaphorical usage of time as a resource. Lakoff and Johnson (1980) have analyzed the metaphorical use of "time is money." The customary metaphorical terms include: "I don't have the time to give you," "How do you spend your time these days?," "You need to budget your time," and "You don't use your time profitably." The point is that all these expressions relate to the use of time as a valuable resource. People employ the money-like concept of time as a means for attaining their goals. This conceptualization of time in monetary terms is explained further:

> Time in our culture is a valuable commodity. It is a limited resource that we use to accomplish our goals. ... Corresponding to the fact that we act as if time is a valuable commodity -- a limited resource, even money -- we conceive of time that way. Thus we understand and experience time as the kind of thing that can be spent, wasted, budgeted, invested wisely or poorly, saved, or squandered. (Lakoff and Johnson, 1980:8)

We should note, though, that this conceptualization is not universal in character, being largely a product of Western culture.

An interesting illustration of how time horizon considerations impact upon decision strategies is given by Prattis (1973), who uses economic anthropology data relating to Rossel Island shell currency from the work of Armstrong (1928). The trade-off between short-term and long-term objectives becomes explicit in the following observations concerning the behavior of the chiefs or limi, who are required to maintain their political position by employing a number of means. Among the means are transactions with purpose-specific shell coins known as ndap (which comes in twenty-two types, ranked by the researcher from the lower denominations, numbered from 1 to 17, having greater liquidity, to the higher denominations, numbered from 18 to 22, having limited usage for specific transactions).

> For all the short-term actions undertaken by limi -- para no racing, song-dances, pig-feasts and circulation of lower value ndap -- the consideration of the costs-payoffs balance appears to be solely in terms of potential payoffs, i.e., a maximax strategy. Para no races were held between chiefs ... and the losers had to pay a winner a No. 18 ndap, which meant that the stakes were very high (Armstrong, 1928:30). ... The circulation and manipulation of the lower ndap coins were designed to keep in motion a series of debtor relations with dependents with a view to reaping short-term profits on interest rates...

> Long-term considerations were characterized by a different strategy. Control and manipulation of the high value ndap were designed mainly to prevent other people from becoming limi. Interest accumulation and immediate profit were forgone in terms of accepting smaller returns in order to buttress existing positions. Armstrong (1928:67) records instances whereby chiefs lent out No. 18 shells to ambitious young men at virtually no interest. These seem to have been attempts to enlist the young men as supporters and to prevent them from becoming rivals. The strategy is one of satisficing in terms of the limi acting in a manner that ensures in a minimal way the achievement of the end -- attainment of power. If a limi

wanted to maximise short-run profit, he could con-
ceivably wait for situations where the No. 18
could be lent out at an exhorbitant rate. But by
preventing future rivalry, the limi satisfices in
his manipulation of the coin, as this appears to
be a minimally acceptable set of conditions
whereby his goal will be reached. (Prattis,
1973:52)

The extended illustration demonstrates that the temporal resource can be used to determine and implement a particular strategic objective. In that sense, time can be
considered as much a virtual meta-resource as money.
Indeed, in the above example, money has been used to place
events (strategic objectives) in the chosen future time
zone. This is an interesting instance of the two meta-resources being exchanged for each other: money now paid cal-
culatingly to strategically fashion a planned political
future.

A similar approach is adopted in the allocation of
resources for relatively faster or slower implementation of
projects. The cost of a project is usually higher if an
accelerated pace is desired. This is tantamount to saying
that an excess of monetary cost is being incurred in
exchange for an economy in the other virtual meta-resource,
namely, the time period for project completion. Any savings
in terms of normal project duration has to be exchanged for
additional resources or a less ambitious project objective.

In an organizational context, this can translated to
trading off planning objectives with planning horizons. The
same objective cannot be attained within a shorter time
period, unless resource commitments are augmented. Hence,
when strategy makers decide upon various strategic alternatives, they in effect weigh the dimensions of these objectives in relation to planning or implementation durations.
Individuals conceive of such planning durations in different
ways, as our research has demonstrated. Some would be looking well into the future, and hence would be weighing the
strategic alternatives differently than others who would be
merely extrapolating near-term conceptions. In whatever way
the negotiating of alternative strategic objectives is carried out, we need to appreciate that planning horizons are
used as trade-off currency for the purpose, although not in
an explicit manner. The characterization of planning horizons as a means for attaining planning objectives can be
appreciated when the horizon is appreciated as a temporal
meta-resource.

THE SILENT POLITICS OF TIME

The finding of this study that the planning horizons considered appropriate by different strategy makers varied significantly according to their individual future time perspectives has managerial implications other than those already discussed. These additional implications have to do with the idea of strategy makers "using" their preferences for particular planning horizons as a means (see preceding section) in their negotiations relating to planning objectives. The usage of temporal orientations as a means, although largely at an unconscious level, is essentially along lines similar to that for the usage of the more common means, such as resources like money, power, and effort.

Much as in the case of a person's proneness to risk-taking, some strategy makers are predisposed to shorter or longer planning periods or to projects of particular durations. This point may be better appreciated by examining the following remarks relating to the implementation of management science proposals:

> Each individual has a time within which he must
> prove the efficacy of his actions -- his personal
> time horizon ... A manager with a shorter horizon
> will prefer problems that have a potential for
> quick resolution, solutions with fast paybacks,
> and projects of a short duration. In our example,
> the client is ambitious and has an operating job
> in a crisis atmosphere; he will lose interest in
> projects which drag on beyond a few months. The
> key is to match the approach to the time horizon
> of the problem and client which has implication
> for project duration and milestones, analytical
> approach, etc. (Hammond, 1979:51)

Given the natural inclination of organizational members to try and influence decisions so as to insure results which are favorable in relation to their individual temporal orientation, as brought out in the above excerpt, there seems to be a valid case for the explicit consideration of individual future orientations while studying organizational decision making.

The organization as a political arena and the phenomenon of power hunger have been the subject of extensive research (Mangham, 1979; Mason and Mitroff, 1983; Mintzberg, 1985; Pettigrew, 1973, 1977). We have noted that people are quite conversant with the nature and use of conventional resources in the negotiation process. There is a clear understanding of the method of assessing the relative worth of the various planning objectives that are potentially available. The underlying measure is generally in the form of financial resource units. Decision making and negotiation of planning objectives seemingly proceed in an uncomplicated manner on the basis of this commonly understood financial metric. This money-like or exchange currency notion of negotiating units is conventionally adopted for assessing alternative planning objectives. Of course, the financial unit metaphor stands for all other quantitative, economic, and tangible forms of negotiable resources that strategy makers employ.

One of the important implications of the findings of this study is that the selection of strategic objectives is influenced in part by the future orientations of the strategy makers. The impact is of course indirect in character. Strategic objectives, as we discussed earlier, are conditioned by individual future orientations. Although strategy makers are not too aware of the dynamics of future orientations, the role of this temporal factor is clearly of some significance in the strategy making process. Temporal compulsions cannot be ignored if one intends to understand and improve the overall process of strategic management.

The battle for short or long periods is almost subterranean. There is an overt negotiation process for strategic planning objectives. There is also, albeit to a lesser degree, some negotiation on planning horizons or implementation periods. However, there is no realization of the silent part played by the individual temporal preferences. Specifically, the executives would not normally be aware that their inherent temporal preferences have covertly driven their choicemaking regarding alternative strategic objectives. This is so because the business training and experience of the strategy makers have predisposed them to formulate strategic objectives principally on the basis of financial and other similar kinds of resources. The significant role of subjective future orientations is rarely recognized. One could well call this phenomenon "the silent politics of time." Being largely of a subtle character, this kind of silent temporal politics needs greater attention from strategy makers.

Although the workings of the temporal imperative are unclear at this stage, it needs to be recognized that the future orientations of individual executives do appear to have a substantive role in strategic management. In particular, the phenomenon of the silent politics of time need to be investigated in some depth within the overall study of strategic decision making.

RESEARCH AND PRACTICE IN STRATEGY MAKING

The comments relating to managerial and research implications have been offered in two separate chapters. Clearly, though, the two areas -- practice and research -- are intrinsically interrelated. Hence, although the observations have been grouped under the two conventional categories, they demand an integrated appreciation. This is particularly critical for ensuring that the research products remain relevant to managerial practice.

As any perceptive researcher working in the management area knows, the all-too-convenient separation of research and practice, in a field such as corporate strategy making, is apt to rob academic inquiry of much that could otherwise be of obvious relevance to both domains. There is much to be said about getting involved in the action, or at least attempting to learn and understand the strategic process through vicarious means, because it is only by studying reactions to prescriptive changes can one better grasp organizational functioning. As Daft (1983:543) has found while reviewing papers, "it becomes painfully clear that many authors have never seen or witnessed the phenomena about which they write." Some effort is clearly needed on the part of researchers to "get into the head" of the strategy makers through such artifices as "transpection" and adoption of multiple perspectives (Bartunek, Gordon, and Weathersby, 1983; Linstone, 1984; Maruyama, 1974).

This justifiably symbiotic relationship between the two worlds of research and practice would be especially evident to the academic researcher who has had the unique experience of having also been a real-life strategy maker in a corporate executive position. This is not to prescribe that all researchers of corporate strategy making should have a spell as a practicing strategy maker, since that would be unattainable almost by definition. For, as a rule, top strategy makers have had to work their way up the organizational hierarchy over fairly extended periods. The point being made here is that the researcher ought to study strategy making, as far as is practicable, on the basis of the experience of real-world strategy makers.

In a cognitive approach to organizational analysis, some progress has been made with studying the cause maps of the subjective environments of organizational members

(Axelrod, 1976; Bateson, 1972; Maruyama, 1963; Steinbruner, 1974; Weick, 1979). Etiographic research methodologies hold promise for unravelling the subjective cause maps of strategic actors. Also, part of the real world experience is usually available in the form of official documents and other archival sources. Qualitative analyses could be carried out with these kinds of data, in order to approach the reality as perceived by the corporate strategy makers.

As a step toward understanding the world of strategy making, the subjective-perceptual approach should be helpful. The role of the temporal dimension is but one facet of this approach. This temporal facet is of course an important one according to this research. But the more significant point is that it is the strategy maker who is the key to the entire strategy making process. Put another way, the most significant factor in strategy making is the strategy maker. A related point can be discerned from some recent research. This research stream highlights the fact that organizations can be considered as reflections of its top managers (Hambrick and Mason, 1984; Kets de Vries and Miller, 1984; Miller, Toulouse, and Belanger, 1985).

However, going beyond the top managers, it is necessary that other employees also be coopted to develop a climate in which strategy making is seen as less esoteric than at present. As the author has argued elsewhere, a "strategic consciousness" needs to be fostered among all categories of organizational members in order to establish a milieu where strategic thinking is a pervasive part of management (Das, 1986). As the organizational level analyses in this study have shown, a distant future orientation, to take one attribute, is not exclusive to the higher echelons. There seems to be no reason why a consciousness about the strategic aspects of corporate management should not be developed among personnel in general, along with such commonly-accepted notions as customer service, quality, innovation, productivity, cost effectiveness, and so forth. Indeed, prescriptions for improving business and management performance have underscored the need for involving various levels of employees in instituting organizational changes and innovations (Kanter, 1983; Leavitt, 1986).

In a general sense, one could see the precursors of the present inquiry in Ewing (1969), McGregor (1960), and Mitroff (1974), who spoke, in their separate ways, about the role of the subjective side in long range planning, management, and science. However, it needs to be clarified that the present investigation places considerably more pronounced emphasis on the role of the individual actor in the overall scheme of things. This inquiry goes farther than the others in professing the significance of the role of the individual in phenomena akin to strategy making, management, and science. This point, as the reader will appreciate, has been one of the foundations of this study, and has consistently informed the analyses and comments.

Furthermore, the subjective side of the strategic actor deserves recognition beyond a few customary remarks at the beginning or end of research papers, as unfortunately has been the common custom. Even when the role of the individual strategic decision maker is recognized as an essential variable for understanding the concept of strategy, the individual is merely mentioned in the introductory scheme of things, as perhaps a possible unit of analysis, and then ignored in the research proper, often on the plea of "space limitations." The "public," interpersonal, organizational, and business dimensions of strategy making have been the dominant concern thus far. This needs to be complemented by a study of the "private," personal, and cognitive aspects of the strategy makers in that strategy making process. Only then the true relevance of such factors as future orientations of strategy makers can be fully appreciated. It is necessary, therefore, to develop a theoretical framework which includes and integrates the private as well as the public aspects of strategy making.

In sum, the strategy maker should be the central focus in a proper study of the strategy making enterprise. The exclusive preoccupation with analyzing objective organizational and environmental data, without accounting for the crucial intervening "conditioning" influence of the subjective side of the strategy makers, can only result in a partial, and hence also potentially misleading, appreciation of corporate strategy making.

APPENDIX A
Survey Questionnaire

<u>PLANNING ORIENTATIONS STUDY</u>

(NOTE: Items not relevant to the research reported in this book have been omitted.)

<u>Name:</u>

<u>Bank</u>: WESTBANK / EASTBANK (whichever appropriate)

1. What is your corporate title?

<u>Circle one</u>

Executive/Senior Vice President	..	3
Vice President	..	2
Assistant Vice President	..	1

2. What is the functional title of your position?

3. What is your major functional area of responsibility?

<u>For WESTBANK Respondents</u>

<u>Circle one</u>

Branch Banking	1
International Banking	2
Corporate Banking	3
Financial Management	4
Credit	5
Staff Support	6
Management Services	7
Automated Data Processing	8
Planning & Marketing	9
Other (Specify)	10

For EASTBANK Respondents

                                    Circle one

                Administration   1
                Credit   2
                Marketing   3
                Operations   4
                Personnel   5
                Product Development   6
                Other (Specify)   7

6. How long have you been working in WESTBANK/EASTBANK?

   Number of years:

10. What do you believe is the most appropriate
    time period for which plans should be drawn up
    in your bank (in terms of performance goals,
    resource allocation, organizational actions,
    etc.) in each of the following areas of
    electronic banking? (This time period should be
    long enough to permit planning for expected growth
    and for changes in strategy, and yet be short enough
    to make reasonably detailed plans possible.)

    The time period you indicate may be either in the
    form of one particular year, such as "3", or a
    range of years, such as "2 to 3" or "9 to 11".

                                    Number of years

    Electronic Funds Transfer

    Electronic Cash Management

    Automated Data Processing Capacity

    Electronic Mail

    Telecommunications

13. Now a somewhat different kind of topic.
On a separate sheet of paper, please list
nine important events you expect to happen in
your own personal life in the future. You only
need to jot down one or two words for each such
expected event for your ease of identification.

After you have listed all nine events,
select the time period that best represents
the occurrence of each event. Indicate this
by circling the appropriate column number:

	Very near future (1)	Near future (2)	Distant future (3)	Very distant future (4)
		Circle one		
Event #1	1	2	3	4
Event #2	1	2	3	4
Event #3	1	2	3	4
Event #4	1	2	3	4
Event #5	1	2	3	4
Event #6	1	2	3	4
Event #7	1	2	3	4
Event #8	1	2	3	4
Event #9	1	2	3	4

14. I would like you to think about how different people
    view the objectives of electronic banking. To what
    extent do you believe the managerial staff in your bank
    are in agreement about the planned objectives
    of electronic banking in each area?

          No agreement at all   .. 1
          Very little agreement   .. 2
          Moderate agreement   .. 3
          Substantial agreement   .. 4
          Complete agreement   .. 5

                                              Circle one

    Electronic Funds Transfer   1 2 3 4 5

    Electronic Cash Management   1 2 3 4 5

    Automated Data Processing Capacity 1 2 3 4 5

    Electronic Mail   1 2 3 4 5

    Telecommunications   1 2 3 4 5

15. Now I would like you to consider the planning period
    for establishing the planned objectives. To what
    extent do you believe the managerial staff in your
    bank are in agreement about the planning period
    for establishing the planned objectives
    in each area? (Please use the same scales
    as in the previous question.)

                                              Circle one

    Electronic Funds Transfer   1 2 3 4 5

    Electronic Cash Management   1 2 3 4 5

    Automated Data Processing Capacity 1 2 3 4 5

    Electronic Mail   1 2 3 4 5

    Telecommunications   1 2 3 4 5

16. There are 3 types of decision strategies that are
used in organizations (standardization, negotiation,
and subjective). These are defined below.
Read the definitions and for each area of electronic
banking indicate which strategy you believe is used
in your bank in dealing with planning matters.
The decision strategies are:

1 -- STANDARDIZATION: a method which is
routine -- standard procedures exist
and are applicable most often.

2 -- NEGOTIATION: a method characterized
by give and take, bargaining, and
negotiation.

3 -- SUBJECTIVE: a method in which people
often have to follow hunches/
intuitions/opinions.

	Standardization (1)	Negotiation (2)	Subjective (3)
		Circle one	
Electronic Funds Transfer	1	2	3
Electronic Cash Management	1	2	3
Automated Data Processing Capacity	1	2	3
Electronic Mail	1	2	3
Telecommunications	1	2	3

17. Sex:　Male　　　　1
　　　　　Female　　　2

18. Year of birth: 19__

19. Indicate your highest level of academic preparation:

<u>Circle one</u>

No high school diploma	1
High school diploma	2
Bachelors degree	3
Masters degree	4
Doctoral degree	5

<u>COMMENTS:</u>

(This is the end of the survey. <u>Thank you very much</u> for your time and cooperation. If you have any comments that you would like to make, please feel free to write them here.)

Your cooperation is greatly appreciated. Please mail your completed questionnaire in the enclosed stamped envelope to:

T.K. Das
Planning Orientations Study
Graduate School of Management
University of California
405 Hilgard Avenue
Los Angeles, CA 90024

APPENDIX B
Statistical Analyses for
the Replication Study

This appendix contains all the tables of statistical analyses relating to the EASTBANK replication sample, as discussed in detail in Chapter 13. The tables follow the same format and sequence as those used in chapters 6 through 12 to present data relating to the main sample (WESTBANK). This identical sequencing of the tables should be convenient in understanding the replication data and statistical results in conjunction with the principal part of the study.

TABLE B.1

Responses by Functional Area and Organizational Level

Functional Area	VP	AVP	Total
1. Administration	0	0	0
2. Credit	1	1	2
3. Marketing	11	8	19
4. Operations	8	11	19
5. Personnel	0	1	1
6. Product Development	4	8	12
7. Other	2	7	9
Organizational Level Total	26	36	62

TABLE B.2

Response Rate Summary

Organizational Level	N	Response Rate (%)
Vice Presidents (VP)	26(74)	35.1
Assistant Vice Presidents (AVP)	36(99)	36.4
Total Overall	62(173)	35.8

Numbers in parentheses represent questionnaires sent out; other numbers indicate usable responses received.

TABLE B.3

Intercorrelation Matrix of all Variables

Variable	(1)ORGLEVEL	(2)FTP	(3)PLGHOR	(4)AGROBJ
(1) ORGLEVEL	1.000	.259*	.038	-.048
(2) FTP	.259*	1.000	.550***	-.210%
(3) PLGHOR	.038	.550***	1.000	.066
(4) AGROBJ	-.048	-.210%	.066	1.000
(5) AGRHOR	-.078	-.421***	-.150	.457***
(6) STANDARD	.118	-.175	-.169%	.338**
(7) NEGOTN	-.169%	.053	.154	-.255*
(8) SUBJECT	.079	.123	.002	-.069

Variable	(5)AGRHOR	(6)STANDARD	(7)NEGOTN	(8)SUBJECT
(1) ORGLEVEL	-.078	.118	-.169%	.079
(2) FTP	-.421***	-.175	.053	.123
(3) PLGHOR	-.150	-.169	-.154	.002
(4) AGROBJ	.457***	.338**	-.255*	-.069
(5) AGRHOR	1.000	.162	-.128	-.026
(6) STANDARD	.162	1.000	-.677***	-.303**
(7) NEGOTN	-.128	-.677***	1.000	-.497***
(8) SUBJECT	-.026	-.303**	-.497***	1.000

% p<.10   * p<.05   ** p<.01   *** p<.001

TABLE B.4

Responses by Demographics and Organizational Level

Demographic Variable	VP	AVP	Total
SEX			
Male	25 (96.2)	27 (75.0)	52 (83.9)
Female	1 (3.8)	9 (25.0)	10 (16.1)
AGE			
Upto 35 years	10 (38.5)	14 (38.9)	24 (38.7)
36 to 50 years	15 (57.7)	20 (55.6)	35 (56.5)
51 years and over	1 (3.8)	2 (5.6)	3 (4.8)
EDUCATION			
High School	2 (7.7)	8 (22.2)	10 (16.1)
Bachelor	15 (57.7)	13 (36.1)	28 (45.2)
Master+Doctor	9 (34.6)	15 (41.7)	24 (38.7)
Organizational Level Total	26	36	62

Numbers in parentheses represent percentages of the
frequencies within each Organizational Level.

TABLE B.5

Job Experience and Organizational Level

Job Experience	VP	AVP	Total
Upto 5 years	5 (19.2)	14 (38.9)	19 (30.6)
6 - 10 years	6 (23.1)	9 (25.0)	15 (24.2)
11 - 15 years	9 (34.6)	5 (13.9)	14 (22.6)
16 - 20 years	1 (3.8)	3 (8.3)	4 (6.5)
21 - 25 years	3 (11.5)	4 (11.1)	7 (11.3)
26 plus years	2 (7.7)	1 (2.8)	3 (4.8)
Total	26 (100.0)	36 (100.0)	62 (100.0)
Mean	12.50	10.31	11.23
S.D.	7.65	8.98	8.45

Numbers in parentheses represent percentages of the frequencies within each Organizational Level.

TABLE B.6

Intercorrelation Matrix of all FTP Variables

Variable	(1) FTP	(2) FTPVNEAR	(3) FTPNEAR	(4) FTPDIST	(5) FTPVDIST
(1) FTP	1.000	_.827***	_.318*	.596***	.696***
(2) FTPVNEAR	-.827***	1.000	_.211%	-.461***	-.379**
(3) FTPNEAR	-.318*	-.211%	1.000	-.582***	-.248*
(4) FTPDIST	.596***	-.461***	-.582***	1.000	-.068
(5) FTPVDIST	.696***	-.379**	-.248*	-.068	1.000

% p<.10   * p<.05   ** p<.01   *** p<.001

TABLE B.7

Percentages of Events in Four Future Time Subzones

Number of events	Very Near	Near	Distant	Very Distant
0	13.7	2.0	3.9	31.4
1	21.6	5.9	13.7	37.3
2	33.3	23.5	23.5	27.5
3	25.5	33.3	29.4	2.0
4	3.9	19.6	15.7	2.0
5	0.0	11.8	11.8	0.0
6	0.0	2.0	0.0	0.0
7	2.0	2.0	2.0	0.0
8	0.0	0.0	0.0	0.0
9	0.0	0.0	0.0	0.0
Total	99	161	145	54
Mean	1.94	3.16	2.84	1.06
S.D.	1.30	1.35	1.45	0.93

The figures for Total, Mean, and S.D. indicate the number of events in each future time subzone.

TABLE B.8

Future Time Perspective and Organizational Level

FTP	VP	AVP	Total
0.00 - 2.00	2 (10.0)	9 (29.0)	11 (21.6)
2.00 - 2.25	6 (30.0)	7 (22.6)	13 (25.5)
2.25 - 2.50	4 (20.0)	7 (22.6)	11 (21.6)
2.50 - 2.75	4 (20.0)	4 (12.9)	8 (15.7)
2.75 plus	4 (20.0)	4 (12.9)	8 (15.7)
Total	20 (100.0)	31 (100.0)	51 (100.0)
Mean S.D.	2.45 0.32	2.26 0.37	2.34 0.36

Numbers in parentheses represent percentages of the
frequencies within each Organizational Level.

TABLE B.9

FTP Variables and Organizational Level

Variable	VP	AVP	Significance Level of T-Tests
FTP	2.450	2.262	.060
N	20	31	
FTPVNEAR	1.600	2.161	n.s.
N	20	31	
FTPNEAR	3.050	3.226	n.s.
N	20	31	
FTPDIST	3.050	2.710	n.s.
N	20	31	
FTPVDIST	1.300	0.903	n.s.
N	20	31	

Significance levels were determined on the basis of two-tailed t-tests using an estimate of separate variance. (Note that the aggregate of the values for the four future time subzones add up to 9 for each Organizational Level.)

TABLE B.10

Preferred Planning Horizons and Organizational Level

PLGHOR	VP	AVP	Total
0.0 - 1.0 year	1 (4.2)	3 (8.6)	4 (6.8)
1.0 - 1.5 years	3 (12.5)	5 (14.3)	8 (13.6)
1.5 - 2.0 years	4 (16.7)	5 (14.5)	9 (15.3)
2.0 - 2.5 years	4 (16.7)	7 (20.0)	11 (18.6)
2.5 - 3.0 years	5 (20.8)	7 (20.0)	12 (20.3)
3.0 - 3.5 years	3 (12.5)	3 (8.6)	6 (10.2)
3.5 - 4.0 years	3 (12.5)	1 (2.9)	4 (6.8)
4.0 plus years	1 (4.2)	4 (11.4)	5 (8.5)
Total	24 (100.0)	35 (100.0)	59 (100.0)
Mean S.D.	2.67 1.19	2.57 1.43	2.61 1.33

Numbers in parentheses represent percentages of the
frequencies within each Organizational Level.

TABLE B.11

Planning Horizon Based on Near vs Distant FTP

| | Preferred Planning Horizon | | Significance |
	Near FTP	Distant FTP	Level of T-Tests
OVERALL	1.946	3.787	.001
N	24	15	
ORGANIZATIONAL LEVEL			
VP	1.800	3.450	.007
N	8	8	
AVP	2.019	4.171	.010
N	16	7	

TABLE B.12

FTP Based on Short vs Long Planning Horizon

| | Future Time Perspective | | Significance |
	Short Plg Hor	Long Plg Hor	Level of T-Tests
OVERALL	2.161	2.647	.001
N	18	11	
ORGANIZATIONAL LEVEL			
VP	2.222	2.667	.038
N	7	5	
AVP	2.121	2.630	.008
N	11	6	

TABLE B.13

Agreement on Planning Objectives and Organizational Level

AGROBJ	VP	AVP	Total
No agreement	0 (0.0)	0 (0.0)	0 (0.0)
Very little agreement	2 (7.7)	0 (0.0)	2 (3.2)
Moderate agreement	8 (30.8)	14 (38.9)	22 (35.5)
Substantial agreement	13 (50.0)	18 (50.0)	31 (50.0)
Complete agreement	3 (11.5)	4 (11.1)	7 (11.3)
Total	26 (100.0)	36 (100.0)	62 (100.0)
Mean S.D.	3.65 0.80	3.72 0.66	3.69 0.72

Numbers in parentheses represent percentages of the frequencies within each Organizational Level.

TABLE B.14

Agreement on Planning Horizons and Organizational Level

AGRHOR	VP	AVP	Total
No agreement	0 (0.0)	1 (2.8)	1 (1.6)
Very little agreement	4 (15.4)	1 (2.8)	5 (8.1)
Moderate agreement	10 (38.5)	17 (47.2)	27 (43.5)
Substantial agreement	11 (42.3)	14 (38.9)	25 (40.3)
Complete agreement	1 (3.8)	3 (8.3)	4 (6.5)
Total	26 (100.0)	36 (100.0)	62 (100.0)
Mean S.D.	3.35 0.80	3.47 0.81	3.42 0.80

Numbers in parentheses represent percentages of the
frequencies within each Organizational Level.

TABLE B.15

Agreement on Planning Objectives and Planning Horizons

	Agreement on		Significance
	Plg Objectives	Plg Horizon	Level of T-Tests
OVERALL	3.694	3.419	.004
N	62	62	
ORGANIZATIONAL LEVEL			
VP	3.654	3.346	.037
N	26	26	
AVP	3.722	3.472	.030
N	36	36	

TABLE B.16

Frequencies of Planning Milieux

| | Planning Milieu | | | |
	I	II	III	IV
OVERALL	25 (40.3)	4 (6.5)	13 (21.0)	20 (32.3)
ORGANIZATIONAL LEVEL				
VP	10 (38.5)	2 (7.7)	6 (23.1)	8 (30.8)
AVP	15 (41.7)	2 (5.6)	7 (19.4)	12 (33.3)

Numbers in parentheses represent percentages of the
frequencies within each Organizational Level.

TABLE B.17

Agreement on Planning Objectives Based on FTP

| | Agreement on Planning Objectives | | Significance |
	Near FTP	Distant FTP	Level of T-Tests
OVERALL	3.667	3.438	n.s.
N	24	10	
ORGANIZATIONAL LEVEL			
VP	3.250	3.375	n.s.
N	8	8	
AVP	3.875	3.500	.072
N	16	8	

TABLE B.18

Agreement on Planning Horizons Based on FTP

| | Agreement on Planning Horizons | | Significance |
	Near FTP	Distant FTP	Level of T-Tests
OVERALL	3.583	2.875	.002
N	24	16	
ORGANIZATIONAL LEVEL			
VP	3.250	3.175	n.s.
N	8	8	
AVP	3.750	2.625	.002
N	16	8	

TABLE B.19

Future Time Perspective in Planning Milieux I and IV

| | Future Time Perspective | | Significance |
	Plg Mil I	Plg Mil IV	Level of T-Tests
OVERALL	2.152	2.450	.003
N	19	19	
ORGANIZATIONAL LEVEL			
VP	2.389	2.431	n.s.
N	6	8	
AVP	2.043	2.465	.002
N	13	11	

TABLE B.20

Frequencies for Planning Milieux and Decision Modes

	Decision Mode Frequencies			
Planning Milieu	Standard ization	Nego tiation	Subjec tive	Total
I. Agreement is High for both Planning Objectives and Planning Horizon (N = 25)	40 32.0 47.6 12.9	59 47.2 39.9 19.0	26 20.8 33.3 8.4	125 40.3
II. Agreement is Low for Planning Objectives and High for Planning Horizon (N = 4)	5 25.0 6.0 1.6	6 30.0 4.1 1.9	9 45.0 11.5 2.9	20 6.5
III. Agreement is High for Planning Objectives and Low for Planning Horizon (N = 13)	26 40.0 31.0 8.4	21 32.3 14.2 6.8	18 27.7 23.1 5.8	65 21.0
IV. Agreement is Low for both Planning Objectives and Planning Horizon (N = 20)	13 13.0 15.5 4.2	62 62.0 41.9 20.0	25 25.0 32.1 8.1	100 32.3
Total (N=62)	84 27.1	148 47.7	78 25.2	310 100.0

Decision Mode frequencies are the totals of number of times respondents in a particular Planning Milieu have indicated a specific mode (the three modes making up a total of 5 for each respondent). The three lines of data for each Planning Milieu are the percentages for rows, columns, and total.

TABLE B.21

Frequencies and Percentages of Decision Modes

Number	Standard ization	Nego tiation	Subjec tive
0	29 (46.8)	13 (21.0)	23 (37.1)
1	9 (14.5)	8 (12.9)	18 (29.0)
2	9 (14.5)	13 (21.0)	10 (16.1)
3	7 (11.3)	9 (14.5)	7 (11.3)
4	4 (6.5)	8 (12.9)	1 (1.6)
5	4 (6.5)	11 (17.7)	3 (4.8)
Total	62 (100.0)	62 (100.0)	62 (100.0)

Numbers in parentheses represent percentages of the frequencies within each Decision Mode.

TABLE B.22

Standardization Mode and Organizational Level

Number	VP	AVP	Total
0	11 (42.3)	18 (50.0)	29 (46.8)
1	3 (11.5)	6 (16.7)	9 (14.5)
2	4 (15.4)	5 (13.9)	9 (14.5)
3	4 (15.4)	3 (8.3)	7 (11.3)
4	2 (7.7)	2 (5.6)	4 (6.5)
5	2 (7.7)	2 (5.6)	4 (6.5)
Total	26 (100.0)	36 (100.0)	62 (100.0)
Mean	1.58	1.19	1.36
S.D.	1.70	1.55	1.61

Numbers in parentheses represent percentages of the
frequencies within each Organizational Level.

TABLE B.23

Negotiation Mode and Organizational Level

Number	VP	AVP	Total
0	7	6	13
	(26.9)	(16.7)	(21.0)
1	6	2	8
	(23.1)	(5.6)	(12.9)
2	3	10	13
	(11.5)	(27.8)	(21.0)
3	3	6	9
	(11.5)	(16.7)	(14.5)
4	3	5	8
	(11.5)	(13.9)	(12.9)
5	4	7	11
	(15.4)	(19.4)	(17.7)
Total	26	36	62
	(100.0)	(100.0)	(100.0)
Mean	2.04	2.64	2.39
S.D.	1.84	1.69	1.77

Numbers in parentheses represent percentages of the frequencies within each Organizational Level.

TABLE B.24

Subjective Mode and Organizational Level

Number	VP	AVP	Total
0	8	15	23
	(30.8)	(41.7)	(37.1)
1	9	9	18
	(34.6)	(25.0)	(29.0)
2	4	6	10
	(15.4)	(16.7)	(16.1)
3	3	4	7
	(11.5)	(11.1)	(11.3)
4	0	1	1
	(0.0)	(2.8)	(1.6)
5	2	1	3
	(7.7)	(2.8)	(4.8)
Total	26	36	62
	(100.0)	(100.0)	(100.0)
Mean	1.39	1.17	1.26
S.D.	1.44	1.32	1.37

Numbers in parentheses represent percentages of the
frequencies within each Organizational Level.

TABLE B.25

Decision Modes and Organizational Level

Decision Mode	VP	AVP	Significance Level of T-Tests
Standardization	1.577	1.194	n.s.
N	26	62	
Negotiation	2.039	2.639	n.s.
N	26	36	
Subjective	1.385	1.167	n.s.
N	26	26	

Significance levels were determined on the basis of two-tailed t-tests using an estimate of separate variance.

TABLE B.26

Planning Milieux and Decision Modes

Decision Mode	Planning Milieu			Significance Level of T-Tests		
	1	2+3	4	1:2+3	1:4	2+3:4
Standardization	1.600	1.824	0.650	n.s.	.011	.016
N	25	17	20			
Negotiation	2.360	1.588	3.100	.064	.088	.003
N	25	17	20			
Subjective	1.040	1.588	1.250	n.s.	n.s.	n.s.
N	25	17	20			

TABLE B.27

Standardization Mode in Planning Milieux I and IV

	Standardization Mode in		Significance
	Plg Mil I	Plg Mil IV	Level of T-Tests
OVERALL	1.600	0.650	.011
N	25	20	
ORGANIZATIONAL LEVEL			
VP	1.400	1.125	n.s.
N	10	8	
AVP	1.733	0.333	.006
N	15	12	

TABLE B.28

Subjective Mode in Planning Milieux I and IV

| | Subjective Mode in | | Significance |
	Plg Mil I	Plg Mil IV	Level of T-Tests
OVERALL	1.040	1.250	n.s.
N	25	20	
ORGANIZATIONAL LEVEL			
VP	0.900	1.625	n.s.
N	10	8	
AVP	1.133	1.000	n.s.
N	15	12	

BIBLIOGRAPHY

Ackoff, Russell L. 1974. Redesigning the Future: A Systems Approach to Societal Problems. New York: Wiley.

Ackoff, Russell L. 1981. Creating the Corporate Future. New York: Wiley.

Adelson, Marvin. 1985. "Bring the future down to earth." Futures Research Quarterly, 1(1):63-73.

Adelson, Marvin, and Samuel Aroni. 1975. "Differential images of the future." In Harold A. Linstone and Murray Turoff (eds.), The Delphi Method: Techniques and Applications, pp. 433-462. Reading, MA: Addison-Wesley.

Agor, Weston H. 1984. Intuitive Management. Englewood Cliffs, NJ: Prentice-Hall.

Aguilar, Francis J. 1967. Scanning the Business Environment. New York: Macmillan.

Aldrich, Howard E. 1979. Organizations and Environments. Englewood Cliffs, NJ: Prentice-Hall.

Alexander, Chris. 1968. Notes Toward a Synthesis of Form. Cambridge, MA: Harvard University Press.

Amara, Roy. 1978. "Probing the future." In Jib Fowles (ed.), Handbook of Futures Research, pp. 41-51. Westport, CT: Greenwood.

Anderson, Carl R., and Frank T. Paine. 1975. "Managerial perceptions and strategic behavior." Academy of Management Journal, 18:811-823.

Andrews, Kenneth R. 1980. The Concept of Corporate Strategy. (rev edn.). Homewood, IL: Irwin.

Ansoff, H. Igor. 1979. Strategic Management. New York: Wiley.

231

Armstrong, J. Scott. 1982. "The value of formal planning for strategic decisions: review of empirical research." Strategic Management Journal, 3:197-211.

Armstrong, W.E. 1928. Rossel Island: An Ethnological Study. Cambridge: Cambridge University Press.

Ascher, William, and William H. Overholt. 1983. Strategic Planning and Forecasting: Political Risk and Economic Opportunity. Somerset, NJ: Wiley.

Ashby, W. Ross. 1968. "Variety, constraint, and the law of requisite variety." In Walter Buckley (ed.), Modern Systems Research for the Behavioral Scientist, pp. 129-136. Chicago: Aldine.

Astley, W. Graham. 1985. "Administrative science as socially constructed truth." Administrative Science Quarterly, 30:497-513.

Axelrod, Robert (ed.). 1976. Structure of Decision: The Cognitive Maps of Political Elites. Princeton, NJ: Princeton University Press.

Ayres, Robert U. 1979. Uncertain Futures: Challenges for Decision Makers. New York: Wiley.

Balderston, Frederick E. 1985. Thrifts in Crisis: Structural Transformation of the Savings and Loan Industry. Cambridge, MA: Ballinger.

Barnard, Chester I. 1938. The Functions of the Executive. Cambridge, MA: Harvard University Press.

Barnes, James H. 1984. "Cognitive biases and their impact on strategic planning." Strategic Management Journal, 5:129-137.

Bartunek, Jean M., Judith R. Gordon, and Rita Preszler Weathersby. 1983. "Developing 'complicated' understanding in administrators." Academy of Management Review, 8:273-284.

Bateson, Gregory. 1972. Steps to an Ecology of Mind. New York: Ballantine.

Bazerman, Max H., and F. David Schoorman. 1983. "A limited rationality model of interlocking directorates." Academy of Management Review, 8:206-217.

Becker, Harold S. 1985. "Making futures research useful: the practitioner's opportunity." Futures Research Quarterly, 1(2):15-28.

Bell, Daniel. 1973. The Coming of Post-Industrial Society: A Venture in Social Forecasting. New York: Basic.

Bell, Wendell, and James A. Mau. 1971. "Images of the future: theory and research strategies." In Wendell Bell and James A. Mau (eds.), The Sociology of the Future: Theory, Cases, and Annotated Bibliography, pp. 6-44. New York: Russell Sage Foundation.

Bennis, Warren G. 1970. "A funny thing happened on the way to the future." In Frances F. Korten, Stuart W. Cook, and John I. Lacey (eds.), Psychology and the Problems of Society, pp. 431-450. Washington, D.C.: American Psychological Association.

Bennis, Warren, and Burt Nanus. 1985. Leaders: The Strategies for Taking Charge. New York: Harper & Row.

Beyer, Janice M. 1981. "Ideologies, values, and decision making in organizations." In Paul C. Nystrom and William H. Starbuck (eds.), Handbook of Organizational Design, Vol. 2, pp. 166-202. New York: Oxford University Press.

Birdwhistell, Ray L. 1970. Kinesics and Context. Philadelphia, PA: University of Pennsylvania Press.

Boniecki, George. 1980. "What are the limits to man's time and space perspectives? - Toward a definition of a realistic planning horizon." Technological Forecasting and Social Change, 17:161-175.

Borsting, Jack R. 1982. "Decision-making at the top." Management Science, 28:341-351.

Boulding, Kenneth E. 1956. "General systems theory: the skeleton of a science." Management Science, 2:197-208.

Boulding, Kenneth E. 1961. The Image: Knowledge in Life and Society. Ann Arbor, MI: University of Michigan Press.

Bourgeois, III, L.J. 1980a. "Performance and consensus." Strategic Management Journal, 1:227-248.

Bourgeois, III, L.J. 1980b. "Strategy and environment: a conceptual integration." Academy of Management Review, 5:25-39.

Bourgeois, III, L.J., and David R. Brodwin. 1984. "Strategic implementation: five approaches to an elusive phenomenon." Strategic Management Journal, 5:241-264.

Bower, Joseph L. 1970. Managing the Resource Allocation Process: A Study of Corporate Planning and Investment. Boston: Division of Research, Graduate School of Business Administration, Harvard University.

Bower, Joseph L., and Yves Doz. 1979. "Strategy formulation: a social and political view." In Dan E. Schendel and Charles W. Hofer (eds.), Strategic Management: A New View of Business Policy and Planning, pp. 152-166. Boston, MA: Little, Brown.

Braybrooke, David, and Charles E. Lindblom. 1970. A Strategy of Decision: Policy Evaluation as A Social Process. New York: Free Press.

Broms, Henri, and Henrik Gahmberg. 1983. "Communication to self in organizations and cultures." Administrative Science Quarterly, 28:482-495.

Brumbaugh, Robert S. 1984. Unreality and Time. Albany, NY: State University of New York Press.

Brunsson, Nils. 1985. The Irrational Organization: Irrationality as a Basis for Organizational Action and Change. New York: Wiley.

Bundy, Robert (ed.). 1976. Images of the Future: The Twenty-First Century and Beyond. Buffalo, NY: Prometheus.

Bunge, Mario. 1973. "The role of forecast in planning." Theory and Decision, 3:207-221.

Camerer, Colin. 1985. "Redirecting research in business policy and strategy." Strategic Management Journal, 6:1-15.

Camillus, John C. 1982. "Reconciling logical incrementalism and synoptic formalism -- an integrated approach to designing strategic planning processes." Strategic Management Journal, 3:277-283.

Carlstein, Tommy, Don Parkes, and Nigel Thrift (eds.). 1978. Making Sense of Time. New York: Wiley.

Carter, E. Eugene. 1971. "The behavioral theory of the firm and top-level corporate decision." Administrative Science Quarterly, 16:413-428.

Chamberlain, Neil W. 1968. Enterprise and Environment: The Firm in Time and Place. New York: McGraw-Hill.

Chandler, Jr., ALfred D. 1962. Strategy and Structure: Chapters in the History of American Industrial Enterprise. Cambridge, MA: MIT Press.

Child, John. 1972. "Organizational structure, environment, and performance: the role of strategic choice." Sociology, 6:1-22.

Child, John. 1974. "What determines organizational performance? The Universals vs. It-all-depends." Organizational Dynamics, Vol. 3 (Summer), pp. 2-18.

Churchman, C. West. 1968. Challenge to Reason. New York: McGraw-Hill.

Clark, Burton. 1972. "The organizational saga in higher education." Administrative Science Quarterly, 17:178-184.

Clark, Peter A. 1978. "Temporal inventories and time structuring in large organizations." In J.T. Fraser, N. Lawrence, and D. Park (eds.), The Study of Time III, pp. 391-416. New York: Springer-Verlag.

Cohen, John. 1954. "The experience of time." Acta Psychologica, 10:207-219.

Cohen, John. 1981. "Subjective time." In J.T. Fraser (ed.), The Voices of Time: A Comparative Survey of Man's Views of Time as Expressed by the Sciences and by the Humanities, 2nd edn., pp. 257-275. New York: George Braziller.

Cohen, Michael D., James G. March, and Johan P. Olsen. 1972. "A garbage can model of organizational choice." Administrative Science Quarterly, 17:1-25.

Cohen, Michael D., James G. March, and Johan P. Olsen. 1976. "People, problems, solutions and the ambiguity of relevance." In James G. March and Johan P. Olsen (eds.), Ambiguity and Choice in Organizations, pp. 24-37. Bergen, Norway: Universitetsforlaget.

Cole, H.S.D. 1977. "Accuracy in the long run -- where are we now?" Omega, 5:529-542.

Cornish, Edward, et al. 1977. The Study of the Future: An Introduction to the Art and Science of Understanding and Shaping of Tomorrow's World. Washington, D.C.: World Future Society.

Cottle, Thomas J. 1968. "The location of experience: a manifest time orientation." Acta Psychologica, 28:129-149.

Cottle, Thomas J. 1969. "The duration inventory: subjective extensions of temporal zones." Acta Psychologica, 29:333-352.

Cottle, Thomas J. 1976. Perceiving Time: A Psychological Investigation with Men and Women. New York: Wiley.

Cottle, Thomas J., and Stephen L. Klineberg. 1974. The Present of Things Future: Explorations of Time in Human Experience. New York: Free Press.

Cummings, L.L. 1982. "Organizational behavior." Annual Review of Psychology, 33:541-579.

Cyert, Richard M., William R. Dill, and James G. March. 1958. "The role of expectations in business decision making." Administrative Science Quarterly, 3:307-340.

Cyert, Richard M., and James G. March. 1963. A Behavioral Theory of the Firm. Englewood Cliffs, NJ: Prentice-Hall.

Daft, Richard L. 1983. "Learning the craft of organizational research." Academy of Management Review, 8:539-546.

Daft, Richard L., and Karl E. Weick. 1984. "Toward a model of organizations as interpretation systems." Academy of Management Review, 9:284-295.

Das, T.K. 1983. "The future dimension in strategy making." Paper presented at the Third Strategic Management Society Conference, Paris, France, October 26-29.

Das, T.K. 1984. "Portmanteau ideas for organizational theorizing." Organization Studies, 5:261-267.

Das, T.K. 1986. "Toward strategic consciousness." Paper presented at the XXVII International Meeting of The Institute of Management Sciences, Gold Coast City, Australia, July 21-23.

Das, T.K. (In process). The Time Dimension in Management: A Guide to Interdisciplinary Literature.

Davis, Stanley M. 1982. "Transforming organizations: the key to strategy in context." Organizational Dynamics, Winter, pp. 64-80.

Dean, Douglas, John Mihalasky, Sheila Ostrander, and Lyn Schroeder. 1974. Executive ESP. Englewood Cliffs, NJ: Prentice-Hall.

Dearborn, DeWitt C., and Herbert A. Simon. 1958. "Selective perception: a note on the departmental identifications of executives." Sociometry, 21:140-144.

de Jouvenel, Bertrand. 1967. The Art of Conjecture. New York: Basic.

Denbigh, Kenneth G. 1981. Three Concepts of Time. New York: Springer-Verlag.

de Volder, M.L., and W. Lens. 1982. "Academic achievement and future time perspective as a cognitive-motivational concept." Journal of Personality and Social Psychology, 42(3):566-571.

Dill, William R. 1958. "Environment as an influence on managerial autonomy." Administrative Science Quarterly, 2:409-443.

Donaldson, Gordon, and Jay W. Lorsch. 1983. Decision Making at the Top. New York: Basic Books.

Doob, Leonard W. 1971. Patterning of Time. New Haven, CT: Yale University Press.

Downey, H. Kirk, Don Hellriegel, and John W. Slocum, Jr. 1977. "Individual characteristics as sources of perceived uncertainty variability." Human Relations, 30:161-174.

Drucker, Peter F. 1972. "Long-range planning means risk-taking." In David W. Ewing (ed.), Long-Range Planning for Management, 3rd edn., pp. 3-19. New York: Harper & Row.

Duncan, Robert B. 1972. "Characteristics of organizational environments and perceived environmental uncertainty." Administrative Science Quarterly, 17:313-327.

Dunne, J.W. 1927. An Experiment with Time. New York: Macmillan.

Ebert, Ronald J., and DeWayne Piehl. 1973. "Time horizon: a concept for management." California Management Review, 15(4):35-41.

Eden, Colin, Sue Jones, and David Sims. 1979. Thinking in Organizations. London: Macmillan.

Eden, Colin, Sue Jones, David Sims, and Tim Smithin. 1981. "The intersubjectivity of issues and issues of intersubjectivity." Journal of Management Studies, 18:37-47.

Edmunds, Stahrl W. 1982. "The role of futures studies in business strategic planning." Journal of Business Strategy, 3(2):40-46.

El Sawy, Omar A. 1983. Temporal Perspective and Managerial Attention: A Study of Chief Executive Strategic Behavior. Unpublished doctoral dissertation, Stanford University.

Emery, Fred E., and Eric L. Trist. 1965. "The causal texture of organizational environments." Human Relations, 18:21-31.

Emery, F.E., and E.L. Trist. 1973. Towards a Social Ecology: Contextual Appreciations of the Future in the Present. London: Plenum.

Emshoff, James, Ian I. Mitroff, and Ralph H. Kilmann. 1978. "The role of idealization in long-range planning: an essay on the logical and socio-emotional aspects of planning." Technological Forecasting and Social Change, 11:335-348.

Encel, Solomon, Pauline K. Marstand, and William Page (eds.). 1975. The Art of Anticipation: Values and Methods in Forecasting. New York: Pica.

Epton, S.R. 1972. "The underestimation of project duration: an explanation in terms of a time-horizon." R & D Management, 2(3):141-142.

Evered, Roger D. 1973. Conceptualizing the Future: Implications for Strategic Management in a Turbulent Environment. Unpublished doctoral dissertation, University of California, Los Angeles.

Ewing, David W. 1969. The Human Side of Planning: Tool or Tyrant? New York: Macmillan.

Ewing, David W. 1972. "The time dimension." In David W. Ewing (ed.), Long-Range Planning for Management, 3rd edn., pp. 439-450. New York: Harper & Row.

Fildes, R., and D. Wood (eds.). 1978. Forecasting and Planning. New York: Praeger.

Forrester, Jay. 1961. Industrial Dynamics. Cambridge, MA: MIT Press.

Forrester, Jay W. 1971. World Dynamics. Cambridge, MA: Wright-Allen.

Fowles, Jib (ed.). 1978. Handbook of Futures Research. Westport, CT: Greenwood.

Fraisse, Paul. 1963. The Psychology of Time. New York: Harper.

Fraisse, Paul. 1981. "Cognition of time in human activity." In Gery d'Ydewalle and Willy Lens (eds.), Cognition in Motivation and Learning, pp. 233-259. Hillsdale, NJ: Erlbaum.

Fraisse, Paul. 1984. "Perception and estimation of time." Annual Review of Psychology, 35:1-36.

Frank, Lawrence K. 1939. "Time perspectives." Journal of Social Philosophy, 4:293-312.

Fraser, Donald R., and James W. Kolari. 1985. The Future of Small Banks in a Deregulated Environment. Cambridge, MA: Ballinger.

Fraser, J.T. 1978. Time as Conflict: A Scientific and Humanistic Study. Basel: Birkhauser Verlag.

Fraser, J.T. (ed.). 1981. The Voices of Time: A Comparative Survey of Man's Views of Time as Expressed by the Sciences and by the Humanities, 2nd edn. New York: George Braziller.

Fraser, J.T., F.C. Haber, and G.H. Muller (eds.). 1972. The Study of Time. New York: Springer-Verlag.

Fraser, J.T., and N. Lawrence (eds.). 1975. The Study of Time II. New York: Springer-Verlag.

Fraser, J.T., N. Lawrence, and D. Park (eds.). 1978. The Study of Time III. New York: Springer-Verlag.

Fraser, J.T., D. Park, and N. Lawrence (eds.). 1981. The Study of Time IV. New York: Springer-Verlag.

Friedman, Yoram, and Eli Segev. 1976. "Horizons for strategic planning." Long Range Planning, 9(5):84-89.

Fujimori, Mitsuo. 1983. "Japanese management philosophies: formation and changes." Keio Business Review, 20:105-116.

Gale, Richard M. (ed.). 1968a. The Philosophy of Time: A Collection of Essays. Atlantic Highlands, NJ: Humanities.

Gale, Richard M. 1968b. The Language of Time. London, UK: Routledge & Kegan Paul.

Gardner, Howard. 1985. The Mind's New Science: A History of the Cognitive Revolution. New York: Basic Books.

Georgiou, Petro. 1973. "The goal paradigm and notes towards a counter paradigm." Administrative Science Quarterly, 18:291-310.

Gerstein, Marc, and Heather Reisman. 1983. "Strategic selection: matching executives to business conditions." Sloan Management Review, Winter, pp. 33-44.

Goodman, Richard Alan. 1967. Organizational Effects Upon Manpower Utilization in Research and Development. Unpublished doctoral dissertation, Graduate School of Business Administration, Washington University, St. Louis, MO.

Goodman, Richard Alan. 1973. "Environmental knowledge and organizational time horizon: some functions and dysfunctions." Human Relations, 26:215-226.

Goodman, Richard Alan, and Anne Sigismund Huff. 1978. "Enriching policy premises for an ambiguous world." In John W. Sutherland (ed.), Management Handbook for Public Administrators, pp. 334-361. New York: Van Nostrand Reinhold.

Gordon, Theodore J., and John Stover. 1976. "Using perceptions and data about the future to improve the simulation of complex systems." Technological Forecasting and Social Change, 9:191-211.

Gorman, Bernard S., and Alden E. Wessman (eds.). 1977. The Personal Experience of Time. New York: Plenum.

Graham, Gerald H. 1968. "Correlates of perceived importance of organizational objectives." Academy of Management Journal, 11:291-300.

Graham, Robert J. 1981. "The role of perception of time in consumer research." Journal of Consumer Research, 7:335-342.

Grant, John H., and William R. King. 1982. The Logic of Strategic Planning. Boston: Little, Brown.

Greenaway, Frank (ed.). 1979. Time and the Sciences. Paris, France: Unesco.

Greenwood, Paul, and Howard Thomas. 1981. "A review of analytical models in strategic planning." Omega, 9:397-417.

Gribbin, John. 1981. Future Worlds. New York: Plenum.

Gurvitch, Georges. 1964. The Sprectrum of Social Time. Dordrecht, Holland: D. Reidel.

Hall, Edward T. 1983. The Dance of Life: The Other Dimension of Time. Garden City, NY: Doubleday.

Hambrick, Donald C., and Phyllis A. Mason 1984. "Upper echelons: the organization as a reflection of its top managers." Academy of Management Review, 9:193-206.

Hamel, Ronald. 1980. "Perception and cognition of the environment." Methodology and Science, 13(2):114-142.

Hammond, III, John S. 1979. "A practitioner-oriented framework for implementation." In R. Doktor, R.L. Schultz, and D.P. Slevin (eds.), The Implementation of Management Science, pp. 35-61. Amsterdam: North-Holland.

Harrison, Edward. 1985. Masks of the Universe. New York: Macmillan.

Hax, Arnaldo C., and Nicolas S. Majluf. 1981. "Toward the formulation of strategic planning: a conceptual framework." Applications of Management Science, 1:213-245.

Hayes, Robert, and William J. Abernathy. 1980. "Managing our way to economic decline." Harvard Business Review, July-August: 67-77.

Hayes-Roth, Barbara, and Frederick Hayes-Roth. 1979. "A cognitive model of planning." Cognitive Science, 3:275-310.

Heirs, B., and Pehrson, G. 1977. The Mind of the Corporation. New York: Harper.

Helmer, Olaf. 1979. "The utility of long-term forecasting." In S. Makridakis and S.C. Wheelwright (eds.), Forecasting, pp. 141-147. Amsterdam: North-Holland.

Hill, J.M.M. 1956. "The time-span of discretion in job analysis." Human Relations, 9:295-323.

Hofer, Charles W., and Dan Schendel. 1978. Strategy Formulation: Analytical Concepts. St. Paul, MN: West.

Hogarth, Robin M. 1980. Judgement and Choice: The Psychology of Decision. Chichester, UK: Wiley.

Hogarth, Robin M., and Spyros Makridakis. 1981. "Forecasting and planning: an evaluation." Management Science, 27:115-138.

Holloway, Clark. 1978. "Does futures research have a corporate role." Long Range Planning, 11(5):17-24.

Homans, George C. 1964. "Bringing men back in." American Sociological Review, 29:309-318.

Hrebiniak, Lawrence G., and William F. Joyce. 1984. Implementating Strategy. New York: Macmillan.

Huber, Bettina J. 1978. "Images of the future." In Jib Fowles (ed.), Handbook of Futures Research, pp. 179-224. Westport, CT: Greenwood.

Hunt, Pearson. 1966. "Fallacy of the one big brain." Harvard Business Review, July-August, pp. 84-90.

Hurst, David K. 1984. "Of boxes, bubbles, and effective management." Harvard Business Review, May-June: 78-88.

Husserl, Edmund. 1964. The Phenomenology of Internal Time-Consciousness (Trans. James S. Churchill). Bloomington, IN: Indiana University Press.

Huxham, C.S., and M.R. Dando. 1981. "Is bounded-vision an adequate explanation of strategic decision-making failures?" Omega, 9:371-379.

Isaack, Thomas S. 1978. "Intuition: an ignored dimension of management." Academy of Management Review, 3:917-922.

Isenberg, Daniel J. 1984. "How senior managers think." Harvard Business Review, November-December, pp. 81-90.

Jacoby, Jacob, George J. Szybillo, and Carol Kohn Berning. 1976. "Time and consumer behavior: an interdisciplinary overview." Journal of Consumer Research, 2:320-339.

Janis, Irving L., and Leon Mann. 1977. Decision Making: A Psychological Analysis of Conflict, Choice, and Commitment. New York: Free Press.

Jaques, Elliott. 1956. Measurement of Responsibility. Cambridge, MA: Harvard University Press.

Jaques, Elliott. 1961. Equitable payment. London: Heinemann.

Jaques, Elliott. 1964. Time-span Handbook. London: Heinemann.

Jaques, Elliott. 1976. A General Theory of Bureaucracy. London: Heinemann.

Jaques, Elliott. 1979. "Taking time seriously in evaluating jobs." Harvard Business Review, September-October, pp. 124-132.

Jaques, Elliott. 1982. The Form of Time. New York: Crane, Russak.

Jemison, David B. 1981. "The importance of an integrative approach to strategic management research." Academy of Management Review, 6:601-608.

Johnson, Gerry. 1985. "Strategic management in action." In Valerie Hammond (ed.), Current Research in Management, pp. 21-38. London: Frances Pinter.

Jones, Thomas E. 1980. Options for the Future: A Comparative Analysis of Policy-Oriented Forecasts. New York: Praeger.

Kahn, Herman, and Anthony J. Wiener. 1967. The Year 2000: A Framework for Speculation on the Next Thirty-Three Years. New York: Macmillan.

Kahneman, Daniel, Paul Slovic, and Amos Tversky (eds.). 1982. Judgment Under Uncertainty: Heuristics and Biases. Cambridge, UK: Cambridge University Press.

Kanter, Rosabeth Moss. 1983. The Change Masters: Innovation for Productivity in the American Corporation. New York: Simon and Schuster.

Kareken, John H. 1986. "Federal bank regulatory policy: a description and some observations." Journal of Business, 59:3-48.

Kastenbaum, Robert. 1961. "The dimensions of future time perspective: an experimental analysis." Journal of General Psychology, 65:203-218.

Katz, Daniel, and Robert L. Kahn. 1978. The Social Psychology of Organizations, 2nd edn. New York: Wiley.

Katz, Ralph. 1980. "Time and work: toward an integrated perspective." Research in Organizational Behavior, 2:81-127.

Kelly, George A. 1958. "Man's construction of his alternatives." In Gordon Lindzey (ed.), Assessment of Human Motives, pp. 33-64. New York: Rinehart.

Kerr, Jeffrey. 1982. "Assigning managers on the basis of the life cycle." Journal of Business Strategy, 2(4):58-65.

Kets de Vries, Manfred F.R., and Danny Miller. 1984. "Neurotic style and organizational pathology." Strategic Management Journal, 5:35-55.

Keys, J. Bernard, and Thomas R. Miller. 1984. "The Japanese management theory jungle." Academy of Management Review, 9:342-353.

Klineberg, Stephen L. 1968. "Future time perspective and the preference for delayed reward." Journal of Personality and Social Psychology, 8:253-257.

Kloeze, H.J., A. Molenkamp, and F.J.W. Roelofs. 1980. "Strategic planning and perticipation: a contradiction in terms?" Long Range Planning, 13(5):10-20.

Kono, Toyohiro. 1984. "Long range planning of U.K. and Japanese corporations: a comparative study." Long Range Planning, 17(2):58-74.

Kotter, John P. 1982a. The General Managers. New York: Free Press.

Kotter, John P. 1982b. "What effective general managers really do." Harvard Business Review, November-December, pp. 156-167.

Lakoff, George, and Mark Johnson. 1980. Metaphors We Live By. Chicago: University of Chicago Press.

Langer, Ellen J. 1975. "The illusion of control." Journal of Personality and Social Psychology, 32:311-328.

Larwood, Laurie, and William Whittaker. 1977. "Managerial myopia: self-serving biases in organizational planning." Journal of Journal of Applied Psychology, 62:194-198.

Lauer, Robert H. 1981. Temporal Man: The Meaning and Uses of Social Time. New York: Praeger.

Lawrence, Paul R., and Jay W. Lorsch. 1967. Organization and Environment: Managing Differentiation and Integration. Cambridge, MA: Harvard University Press.

Leavitt, Harold J. 1986. Corporate Pathfinders: Building Vision and Values into Organizations. Homewood, IL: Dow Jones-Irwin.

Leemhuis, J.P. 1985. "Using scenarios to develop strategies." Long Range Planning, 18(2):30-37.

Leibenstein, Harvey. 1979. "A branch of economics is missing: micro-micro theory." Journal of Economic Literature, 17:477-502.

Lenz, R.T. 1981. "'Determinants' of organizational performance: an interdisciplinary review." Strategic Strategic Management Journal, 2:131-154.

Lenz, R.T., and Jack L. Engledow. 1986. "Environmental analysis units and strategic decision-making: a field study of selected 'leading-edge' corporations." Strategic Management Journal, 7:69-89.

Leontiades, Milton. 1982. "Choosing the right manager to fit the strategy." Journal of Business Strategy, 3(2):58-69.

Lessing, Elise E. 1968. "Demographic, developmental and personality correlates of length of future time perspective (FTP)." Journal of Personality, 36:183-201.

Levine, Sol, and Paul E. White. 1961. "Exchange as a conceptual framework for the study of interorganizational relationships." Administrative Science Quarterly, 5:583-601.

Lewin, Kurt. 1951. Field Theory in Social Science: Some Theoretical Papers. New York: Harper.

Lindblom, Charles E. 1959. "The science of 'muddling through'." Public Administration Review, 19:79-88.

Lindblom, Charles E. 1968. The Policy Making Process. Englewood Cliffs, NJ: Prentice-Hall.

Lindblom, Charles E. 1979. "Still muddling, not yet through." Public Administration Review, 39:517-526.

Linder, Stephen H. 1982. "Perceptions of the policy-making environment: cognitive differences among administrators in five federal agencies." Human Relations, 35:463-490.

Linstone, Harold A. 1973. "On discounting the future." Technological Forecasting and Social Change, 4:335-338.

Linstone, Harold A. 1977. "Confessions of a forecaster." In Harold A. Linstone and W.H. Clive Simmonds (eds.), Futures Research: New Directions, pp. 3-12. Reading, MA: Addison-Wesley.

Linstone, Harold A. 1984. Multiple Perspectives for Decision Making: Bridging the Gap Between Analysis and Action. New York: Elsevier.

Linstone, Harold A., and W.H. Clive Simmonds (eds.). 1977. Futures Research: New Directions. Reading, MA: Addison-Wesley.

Lorange, Peter. 1980. Corporate Planning: An Executive Viewpoint. Englewood Cliffs, NJ: Prentice-Hall.

Lorange, Peter. 1982. Implementation of Strategic Planning. Englewood Cliffs, NJ: Prentice-Hall.

Lorsch, Jay W., and John J. Morse. 1974. Organizations and Their Members: A Contingency Approach. New York: Harper.

Loye, David. 1978. The Knowable Future: A Psychology of Forecasting and Prophecy. New York: Wiley.

Lyles, Marjorie A., and Ian I. Mitroff. 1985. "The impact of sociopolitical influences on strategic problem formulation." Advances in Strategic Management, 3:69-81.

MacCrimmon, Kenneth R., and Ronald N. Taylor. 1976.
"Decision making and problem solving." In Marvin D.
Dunnette (ed.), Handbook of Industrial and Organizational
Psychology, pp. 1397-1453. Chicago: Rand McNally.

MacCrimmon, Kenneth R., and Donald A. Wehrung. 1986. Taking
Risks: The Management of Uncertainty. New York: Free
Press.

MacMillan, Ian C., and William D. Guth. 1985. "Strategy
implementation and middle management coalitions."
Advances in Strategic Management, 3:233-254.

Makridakis, Spyros, and Steven C. Wheelwright. 1981.
"Forecasting an organization's futures." In Paul C.
Nystrom and William H. Starbuck (eds.), Handbook of
Organizational Design, Vol. 1, pp. 122-138. New York:
Oxford University Press.

Malaska, Pentti. 1985. "Multiple scenario approach and
strategic behavior in European companies." Strategic
Management Journal, 6:339-355.

Mangham, Iain. 1979. The Politics of Organizational Change.
Westport, CT: Greenwood Press.

March, James G. 1962. "The business firm as a political
coalition." Journal of Politics, 24:662-678.

March, James G. 1976. "The technology of foolishness." In
James G. March and Johan P. Olsen (eds.), Ambiguity and
Choice in Organizations, pp. 69-81. Bergen, Norway:
Universitetsforlaget.

March, James G. 1981. "Decisions in organizations and
theories of choice." In Andrew H. Van de Ven and William
F. Joyce (eds.), Perspectives on Organization Design and
Behavior, pp. 205-244. New York: Wiley Interscience.

March, James G., and Johan P. Olsen. 1976. "Attention and
the ambiguity of self-interest." In James G. March and
Johan P. Olsen (eds.), Ambiguity and Choice in
Organizations, pp. 38-53. Bergen, Norway:
Universitetsforlaget.

March, James G., and Herbert A. Simon. 1958. Organizations.
New York: Wiley.

Marcus, Stephen Keith. 1976. Jungian Typology and Time Orientation. Unpublished doctoral dissertation, United States International University.

Maruyama, Magoroh. 1963. "The second cybernetics: deviation-amplifying mutual causal processes." American Scientist, 51:164-179.

Maruyama, Magoroh. 1974. "Paradigms and communication." Technological Forecasting and Social Change, 6:3-32.

Maruyama, Magoroh. 1982. "New mindscapes for future business policy and management." Technological Forecasting and Social Change, 21:53-76.

Mason, Richard O., and Ian I. Mitroff. 1983. "A teleological power-oriented theory of strategy." Advances in Strategic Management, 2:31-41.

May, Graham. 1982. "The argument for more future-oriented planning." Futures, 14:313-318.

McCaskey, Michael B. 1976. "Tolerance for ambiguity and the perception of environmental uncertainty in organization design." In Ralph H. Kilmann, Louis R. Pondy, and Dennis P. Slevin (eds.), The management of The Management of Organization Design, Vol. 2, pp. 59-85. New York: Elsevier North-Holland.

McGrath, Joseph E., and Nancy L. Rotchford. 1983. "Time and behavior in organizations." Research in Organizational Behavior, 5:57-101.

McGregor, Douglas. 1960. The Human Side of Enterprise. New York: McGraw-Hill.

McHale, John. 1969. The Future of the Future. New York: Braziller.

McKenney, James L., and Peter G.W. Keen. 1974. "How managers' minds work." Harvard Business Review, May-June, pp. 79-90.

McMillan, Charles J. 1980. "Qualitative models of organisational decision-making." Journal of General Management, 5(4):22-39.

McTaggart, J.M.E. 1968. The Nature of Existence, Vol. II (Ed. C.D. Broad). Cambridge, UK: Cambridge University Press.

Meadows, Donella H., Dennis L. Meadows, Jorgen Randers, and William W. Behrens, III. 1972. The Limits to Growth: A Report for the Club of Rome's Project on the Predicament of Mankind. New York: Universe.

Mellor, D.H. 1981. Real Time. Cambridge, UK: Cambridge University Press.

Meyer, Marshall W. 1975. "Organizational domains." American Sociological Review, 40:599-615.

Michon, John A., and Janet L. Jackson (eds.). 1985. Time, Mind, and Behavior. New York: Springer-Verlag.

Miles, Raymond E., Charles E. Snow, and Jeffrey Pfeffer. 1974. "Organization-environment: concepts and issues." Industrial Relations, 13:244-264.

Miller, D.T. 1976. "Ego involvement and attributions for success and failure." Journal of Personality and Social Psychology, 34:901-906.

Miller, Danny, and Peter H. Friesen. 1983. "Strategy-making and environment: the third link." Strategic Management Journal, 4:221-235.

Miller, Danny, Manfred F.R. Kets de Vries, and Jean-Marie Toulouse. 1982. "Top executive locus of control and its relationship to strategy-making, structure, and environment." Academy of Management Journal, 25:237-253.

Miller, Danny, Jean-Marie Toulouse, and Noel Belanger. 1985. "Top executive personality and corporate strategy: three tentative types." Advances in Strategic Management, 3:223-232.

Miller, Eric J. 1959. "Technology, territory, and time." Human Relations, 12:243-272.

Miller, George A. 1956. "The magical number seven, plus or minus two: some limits on our capacity for processing information." Psychological Review, 63:81-97.

Mintzberg, Henry. 1976. "Planning on the left side and managing on the right." Harvard Business Review, July-August, pp. 49-58.

Mintzberg, Henry. 1985. "The organization as a political arena." Journal of Management Studies, 22:133-154.

Mintzberg, Henry, Duru Raisinghani, and Andre Theoret. 1976. "The structure of 'unstructured' decision processes." Administrative Science Quarterly, 21:246-275.

Mintzberg, Henry, and James A. Waters. 1983. "The mind of the strategist(s)." In Suresh Srivastva and Associates, The Executive Mind: New Insights on Managerial Thought and Action, pp. 58-83. San Francisco, CA: Jossey-Bass.

Mitroff, Ian I. 1974. The Subjective Side of Science: A Philosophical Inquiry into the Psychology of the Apollo Moon Scientists. New York: Elsevier.

Mitroff, Ian I. 1983. Stakeholders of the Organizational Mind. San Francisco, CA: Jossey-Bass.

Mitroff, Ian I., and Richard O. Mason. 1983. "The stakeholders of executive decision making." In Suresh Srivastva and Associates, The Executive Mind: New Insights on Managerial Thought and Action, pp. 144-168. San Francisco, CA: Jossey-Bass.

Montanari, John R. 1978. "Managerial discretion: an expanded model of organization choice." Academy of Management Academy of Management Review, 3:231-241.

Morgan, Gareth. 1983. "Rethinking corporate strategy: a cybernetic perspective." Human Relations, 36:345-360.

Morris, Richard. 1984. Time's Arrows: Scientific Attitudes Toward Time. New York: Simon and Schuster.

Morrison, James L., William L. Renfro, and Wayne I. Boucher (eds.). 1983. Applying Methods and Techniques of Futures Research. San Francisco, CA: Jossey-Bass.

Muller, Herbert J. 1974. Uses of the Future. Bloomington, IN: Indiana University Press.

Murray, Jr., Edwin A. 1978. "Strategic choice as a negotiated outcome." Management Science, 24:960-972.

Naisbitt, John. 1982. Megatrends: Ten New Directions Transforming Our Lives. New York: Warner.

Nalbandian, John, and Donald E. Klingner. 1980. "Integrating context and decision strategy: a contingency theory approach to public personnel administration." Administration Administration & Society, 12:178-202.

Navon, David. 1978. "On a conceptual hierarchy of time, space, and other dimensions." Cognition, 6:223-228.

Naylor, Thomas H. 1983. "Strategic planning and forecasting." Journal of Forecasting, 2:109-118.

Neisser, Ulric. 1976. Cognition and Reality: Principles and Implications of Cognitive Psychology. San Francisco, CA: W.H. Freeman.

Neustadt, Richard E., and Ernest R. May. 1986. Thinking in Time: The Uses of History for Decision Makers. New York: Free Press.

Newton-Smith, W.H. 1980. The Structure of Time. London: Routledge & Kegan Paul.

Nottenburg, Gail, and Donald B. Fedor. 1983. "Scarcity in the environment: organizational perceptions, interpretations and responses." Organization Studies, 4:317-337.

Nuttin, Joseph R. 1964. "The future time perspective in human motivation and learning." Acta Psychologica, 23:60-82.

Nystrom, Paul C., and William H. Starbuck. 1984. "To avoid organizational crises, unlearn." Organizational Dynamics, Spring, pp. 53-65.

Ohmae, Kenichi. 1982. The Mind of the Strategist: The Art of Japanese Business. New York: McGraw-Hill.

Orme, J.E. 1969. Time, Experience and Behaviour. New York: American Elsevier.

Ornstein, Robert E. 1970. On the Experience of Time. Baltimore, MD: Penguin.

Paskins, David. 1985. "Planning horizons and organisational strata." In Valerie Hammond (ed.), Current Research in Management, pp. 70-83. London: Frances Pinter.

Perelman, Lewis J. 1980. "Time in system dynamics." In Augusto A. Legasto, Jr., Jay W. Forrester, and James M. Lyneis (eds.), System Dynamics, pp. 75-89. Amsterdam: North-Holland.

Perrow, Charles. 1980. "'Zoo story' or 'Life in the organizational sandpit'." In Graeme Salaman and Kenneth Thompson (eds.), Control and Ideology in Organizations, pp. 259-277. Cambridge, MA: MIT Press.

Peters, Thomas J. 1982. "The rational model has led us astray." Planning Review, 10(2):16-23.

Peters, Thomas J., and Robert H. Waterman, Jr. 1982. In Search of Excellence: Lessons From America's Best-Run Companies. New York: Harper and Row.

Pettigrew, Andrew M. 1973. The Politics of Organisational Decision-Making. London: Tavistock.

Pettigrew, Andrew M. 1977. "Strategy formulation as a political process." International Studies of Management and Organization, 7(2):78-87.

Pfeffer, Jeffrey, and Gerald R. Salancik. 1978. The External Control of Organizations: A Resource Dependence Perspective. New York: Harper.

Polak, Fred. 1973. The Image of the Future. Amsterdam: Elsevier Scientific.

Polanyi, Michael. 1967. The Tacit Dimension. New York: Doubleday.

Pondy, Louis R. 1984. "Union of rationality and intuition in management action." In Suresh Srivastva and Associates, The Executive Mind: New Insights on Managerial Thought and Action, pp. 169-191. San Francisco, CA: Jossey-Bass.

Pondy, Louis R., and David M. Boje. 1980. "Bringing mind back in." In William M. Evan (ed.), Frontiers in Organization and Management, pp. 83-101. New York: Praeger.

Pondy, Louis R., and Ian I. Mitroff. 1979. "Beyond open system models of organization." In Barry M. Staw and Larry L. Cummings (eds.), Research in Organizational Behavior, Vol. 1, pp. 3-39. Greenwich, CT: JAI Press.

Porter, Lyman W. 1958. "Differential self-perceptions of management personnel and line workers." Journal of Applied Psychology, 42:105-108.

Prattis, J.I. 1973. "Strategising man." Man, 8:46-58.

Quinn, James Brian. 1980. Strategies for Change: Logical Incrementalism. Homewood, IL: Irwin.

Radford, K.J. 1980. Strategic Planning: An Analytical Approach. Reston, VA: Reston.

Reichenbach, Hans. 1971. The Direction of Time. Berkeley, CA: University of California Press.

Ronchi, Luciano. 1980. "Strategic adaptation as a partially rational process." Omega, 8:661-670.

Rowan, Roy. 1986. The Intuitive Manager. Boston, MA: Little, Brown.

Sapp, Richard W. 1980. "Banks look ahead: a survey of bank planning." The Magazine of Bank Administration, 56(7):33-40.

Saunders, Anthony, and Lawrence J. White. 1986. Technology and the Regulation of Financial Markets: Securities, Futures, and Banking. Lexington, MA: D.C. Heath.

Schon, Donald A. 1983. The Reflective Practitioner: How Professionals Think in Action. New York: Basic Books.

Schulman, Paul R. 1976. "The reflexive organization: on decisions, boundaries and the policy process." The Journal of Politics, 38:1014-1023.

Schutz, Alfred. 1962. Collected Papers. The Hague, Netherlands: Nijhoff.

Schutz, Alfred. 1967. The Phenomenology of the Social
World. Evanston, IL: Northwestern University Press.

Schwenk, Charles R. 1985. "Management illusions and biases:
Their impact on strategic decisions." Long Range
Planning, 18(5):74-80.

Settle, Robert B., Pamela Alreck, and Michael A. Belch.
1981. "F-A-S-T: a standardized measure of temporics."
Paper submitted to the American Psychological Association
Annual Convention, Los Angeles, August.

Sherover, Charles M. 1975. The Human Experience of Time:
The Development of its Philosophic Meaning. New York:
York University Press.

Silverman, David. 1970. The Theory of Organizations: A
Sociological Framework. London: Heinemann.

Simon, Herbert A. 1970. The Sciences of the Artificial.
Cambridge, MA: MIT Press.

Simon, Herbert A. 1973. "The structure of ill-structured
problems." Artificial Intelligence, 4:181-201.

Simon, Herbert A. 1976. Administrative Behavior: A Study of
Decision-Making Processes in Administrative Organization,
3rd edn. New York: Free Press.

Simon, Herbert A. 1979. Models of Thought. New Haven, CT:
Yale University Press.

Sims, Jr., Henry P., and Dennis A. Gioia, and Associates.
1986. The Thinking Organization: Dynamics of
Organizational Social Cognition. San Francisco, CA:
Jossey-Bass.

Smircich, Linda, and Charles Stubbart. 1985. "Strategic
management in an enacted world." Academy of Management
Review, 10:724-736.

Smith, Gilbert, and David May. 1980. "The artificial debate
between rationalist and incrementalist models of decision
making." Policy and Politics, 8:147-161

Sontheimer, Kevin C., and Richard S. Thorn. 1986.
"Competitive strategies in U.S. banking." Long Range
Planning, 19(1):113-120.

Starbuck, William H. 1976. "Organizations and their environments." In Marvin D. Dunnette (ed.), Handbook of Industrial and Organizational Psychology, pp. 1069-1123. Chicago: Rand McNally.

Steinbruner, John D. 1974. The Cybernetic Theory of Decision. Princeton, NJ: Princeton University Press.

Steiner, George A. 1969. Top Management Planning. New York: Macmillan.

Steiner, George A. 1979. "Contingency theories of strategy and strategic management." In Dan E. Schendel and Charles W. Hofer (eds.), Strategic Management: A New View of Business Policy and Planning, pp. 405-416. Boston, MA: Little, Brown.

Stinchcombe, Arthur L. 1974. Creating Efficient Industrial Administrations. New York: Academic Press.

Stonich, Paul J. 1984. "The performance measurement and reward system: critical to strategic management." Organizational Dynamics, Winter, pp. 45-57.

Strauch, Ralph E. 1975. "'Squishy' problems and quantitative methods." Policy Sciences, 6:175-184.

Taschdjian, Edgar. 1977. "Time horizon: the moving boundary." Behavioral Science, 22:41-48.

Taylor, Bernard, and Kevin Hawkins (eds.). 1972. A Handbook of Strategic Planning. London: Longman.

Taylor, Ronald N. 1976. "Psychological aspects of planning." Long Range Planning, 9(2):66-74.

Thomae, Hans. 1981. "Future time perspective and the problem of cognition/motivation interaction." In Gery d'Ydewalle and Willy Lens (eds.), Cognition in Human Motivation and Learning, pp. 261-274. Hillsdale, NJ: Erlbaum.

Thompson, James D. 1964. "Decision-making, the firm, and the market." In W.W. Cooper et al (eds.), New Perspectives in Organization Research, pp. 334-348. New York: Wiley.

Thompson, James D. 1967. Organizations in Action. New York: McGraw-Hill.

Thompson, James D., and William J. McEwen. 1958. "Organizational goals and environment: goal setting as an interaction process." American American Sociological Review, 23:23-31.

Thompson, James D., and Arthur Tuden. 1959. "Strategies, structures, and processes of organizational decision." In James D. Thompson, Peter B. Hammond, Robert W. Hawkes, Buford H. Junker, and Arthur Tuden (eds.), Comparative Studies in Administration, pp. 195-216. Pittsburgh, PA: University of Pittsburgh Press.

Tilles, Seymour. 1963. "How to evaluate corporate strategy." Harvard Business Review, July-August, pp. 111-121.

Toffler, Alvin. 1971. Future Shock. New York: Bantam.

Toffler, Alvin (ed.). 1974. Learning for Tomorrow: The Role of the Future in Education. New York: Random House.

Toffler, Alvin. 1981. The Third Wave. New York: Bantam.

Toulmin, Stephen, and June Goodfield. 1982. The Discovery of Time. Chicago, IL: The University of Chicago Press.

Tregoe, Benjamin B., and John W. Zimmerman. 1980. Top Management Strategy: What it is and How to Make it Work. New York: Simon and Schuster.

Twiss, Brian C. 1980. Managing Technological Innovation, 2nd edn. London: Longman.

Utterback, James M. 1979. "Environmental analysis and forecasting." In Dan E. Schendel and Charles W. Hofer (eds.), Strategic Management: A New View of Business Policy and Planning, pp. 134-144. Boston, MA: Little, Brown.

van Cauwenbergh, A., and N. van Robaeys. 1980. "The functioning of management at the corporate level." Journal of General Management, 5(3):19-29.

van Fraassen, Bas C. 1978. "Time: physical and experienced." Epistemologia, 1:323-336.

Vickers, Geoffrey. 1965. The Art of Judgment: A Study of Policy Making. New York: Basic Books.

Wack, Pierre. 1985. "Scenarios: uncharted waters ahead." Harvard Business Review, September-October, pp. 73-89.

Wagner, III, John A. 1978. "The organizational double bind: toward an understanding of rationality and its complement." Academy of Management Review, 3:786-795.

Wallace, Melvin, and Albert I. Rabin. 1960. "Temporal experience." Psychological Bulletin, 57:213-236.

Watzlawick, Paul, Janet Helmick Beavin, and Don D. Jackson. 1967. Pragmatics of Human Communication: A Study of Interactional Patterns, Pathologies, and Paradoxes. New York: Norton.

Watzlawick, Paul, John H. Weakland, and Richard Fisch. 1974. Change: Principles of Problem Formation and Problem Resolution. New York: Norton.

Weick, Karl E. 1977. "Re-punctuating the problem." In Paul S. Goodman, Johannes M. Pennings, and Associates (eds.), New Perspectives on Organizational Effectiveness, pp. 193-225. San Francisco, CA: Jossey-Bass.

Weick, Karl E. 1979. The Social Psychology of Organizing, 2nd edn. Reading, MA: Addison-Wesley.

Weick, Karl E. 1984. "Managerial thought in the context of action." In Suresh Srivastva and Associates, The Executive Mind: New Insights on Managerial Thought and Action, 221-242. pp. 221-242. San Francisco, CA: Jossey-Bass.

Weick, Karl E., and Richard L. Daft. 1983. "The effectiveness of interpretation systems." In Kim S. Cameron and David A. Whetten (eds.), Organizational Effectiveness: A Comparison of Multiple Models, pp. 71-93. New York: Academic.

Wheelwright, Steven C., and Robert L. Banks. 1979. "Involving operating managers in planning process evolution." Sloan Management Review, 20(4):43-59.

Whitrow, G.J. 1980. The Natural Philosophy of Time, 2nd edn. New York: Oxford University Press.

Wissema, J.G., H.W. van der Pol, and H.M. Messer. 1980. "Strategic management archetypes." Strategic Management Journal, 1:37-47.

Wrapp, H. Edward. 1967. "Good managers don't make policy decisions." Harvard Business Review, September-October, pp. 91-99.

Wright, William F. 1980. "Cognitive information processing biases: implications for producers and users of financial information." Decision Sciences, 11:284-298.

Yaker, Henri, Humphrey Osmond, and Frances Cheek (eds.). 1972. The Future of Time: Man's Temporal Environment. Garden City, NY: Anchor.

Yuchtman, Ephraim, and Stanley Seashore. 1967. "A system resource approach to organizational effectiveness." American Sociological Review, 32:891-903.

Zentner, Rene D. 1982. "Scenarios: past, present and future." Long Range Planning, 15(3):12-20.

AUTHOR INDEX

SUBJECT INDEX

ABOUT THE AUTHOR

T.K. DAS is Assistant Professor of Strategic Management in the College of Business Administration, Texas Tech University, and Faculty Associate at the Texas Center for Productivity and Quality of Work Life. He has also taught at the California State University at Los Angeles.

Professor Das has a Ph.D. in Management Strategy and Policy from the Graduate School of Management, University of California at Los Angeles (UCLA). He also holds two master's degrees in Management and Mathematics and a bachelor's degree in Physics.

He has had extensive experience as a bank executive. One of his major responsibilities at the corporate level was the strategic, organization-wide transformation of one of the world's largest commercial banking organizations (which forms the basis of a book he is now completing).

Dr. Das has published over 80 articles in scholarly and professional journals. He is the author of several books and monographs, and has recently co-edited the two-volume Human Resource Management and Productivity: State of the Art and Future Prospects. In addition, he has read papers and chaired sessions in various academic and professional conferences.

His current research involvements include the "Project on Executive Thinking," role of top executives in the strategic management process, strategic transformation of large organizations, strategic consciousness, future orientations of executives, time dimension in management, new thinking frameworks for executives to foster creativity in decision making, and the preferences of executives for various principles of ethical conduct.

DATE DUE

GAYLORD			PRINTED IN U.S.A